SOS

RWANDA'S 30-YEAR APOCALYPSE

SOS - RWANDA'S 30-YEAR APOCALYPSE

Scripture quotations taken from the New American Standard Bible® (NASB), Copyright © 1960, 1962, 1963, 1968, 1971, 1972, 1973, 1975, 1977, 1995 by The Lockman Foundation
Used by permission. www.Lockman.org

Published by Fig Factor Media, LLC.
Printed in the United States of America
Cover Design and Layout by Juan Pablo Ruiz

ISBN: 978-1-7345680-3-5
Library of Congress Control Number: **2020906240**

*Finally, He will cause
justice to be victorious*

—Matthew 12:20

Dedicated to Kizito Mihigo

The Mozart of Africa.
The apostle of peace and reconciliation.
In the midst of Rwanda injustice and excessive cruelty,
Few followed God as faithfully.
Very few held on so firmly.

Justice miscarried.
Beaten bloody and tortured,
You looked death in the face and didn't flinch.
You died a martyr.
Left a model of nobility and
Unforgettable example of virtue for the whole world.
Through you and thousands of other Kizitos,
May there be an end to Rwanda's 30-Year Apocalypse.
RIP – Saint Kizito Mihigo
Your spirit lives on, now and forever more.

"For this reason, you survived
To make known the truth to the world.
What you have seen, heard, and experienced,
Proclaim it to the whole world.
The testimonies entrusted to you,
Shout it from the rooftops.
What the Rwandan martyrs – your very own brethren
– handed over to you
Before being brutally murdered
While their rights and voice were taken away,
Silenced and killed like something that has no value,
You must make it known to the end of the earth!
I am calling you to be their voice! I am calling you to
be their scribe!
For it is this reason you were born, survived the wars
and the Genocides,
To proclaim the truth they were not allowed to share.
I am Almighty God! I will give wings to this message.
It will reach to the end of the earth."

CONTENTS:

SOS

For the past few months, our organization was contacted by different Rwandans: nurses, mothers, and concerned friends sounding the alarm that there is a possible medical genocide taking place inside Rwanda's hospitals. Though these people did not know each other, they all told us similar stories, saying, "Certain agents in the medical field have received orders from above to kill, especially male Hutus who would come to be seen."

The last message from a concerned mother read, "Early in March 2020, three Hutu young men, graduates of Rwanda University, died after being given an injection. All they had was malaria but the next moment, they were dead! Their names are: Jean Luke Hitimana, Dieudone Mukeshimana and Manishimwe Mukunzi."

Through this book, I am sounding the alarm, calling powerful nations, the United Nations (UN), and international community organizations to investigate these things.

The UN tells us, "By **1994**, Rwanda's population stood at **more than 7 million people** comprised of **three ethnic groups**: the Hutu (who made up roughly 85 percent of the population), the Tutsi (14 percent), and the Twa (1 percent)."[1]

After hearing the heartbreaking stories, I too, am sounding the alarm asking two things:

1. A prompt, thorough, independent investigation where Rwanda Citizens, whose right to speech have been stolen, be allowed to talk freely to independent investigators without the Rwanda government's presence.

2. A census to show where the statistics of male Hutus stand now compared to the year 1994.

Rwandan Hutus children at Nyamata Hospital. There is no room for them in the inn. Tutsi children however will be received and hospitalized inside, whether they have health insurance or not. Photo taken early in 2020.

INTRODUCTION

THE OTHER SIDE OF THE STORY

Imagine if Hitler had won the war and then lied, proclaiming himself a hero who stopped the war and a savior of those who survived the Holocaust? Imagine that during the Holocaust there was no presence of an international community to report on his crimes in the war zone! Imagine if, through means of great deceit and intrigue, he played the card so well that he was the only one allowed to tell the story of the Holocaust to the rest of the world! Imagine what kind of story he would have to tell!

Imagine that this Hitler operated behind the scenes while his men did the dirty job of eliminating the Jews and anyone who stood in his way. He operated shrewdly, like the serpent, and in the end he told the survivors, "I am sorry for the loss of your loved ones but, actually, I stopped the war and I came to rescue you and now I am your new king!"

Imagine the survivors who did not see him in action beginning to believe in their new savior and thanking him for the rescue! Who, using fear and intimidation, took the rights of the citizens, shepherd them with a gun, silenced the intellectual and the learned who knew the truth of his evil deeds, and said, "Keep your mouth shut. If you dare to say anything, if you ever speak up, I will label you a 'genocidaire' and charge you with genocide/

holocaust ideology under the new law I just implemented."

Imagine that he also won the heart of powerful nations who, after failing to be present during the massacres, feel they owe him an apology and are obligated to support him. Imagine a man who controls the executive, judiciary and legislative branches. Imagine the story he made up to cover up his own crimes!

Today, I have come to tell you the true story – not the twisted version of Hitler! I will tell you what I have seen and experienced. I will share the testimonies of the martyrs and those whose rights to speak have been taken away.

I ask you to read this book with an open mind and great grace. It is a book of the strong and not for the weak. I am going to take you through 30 years of Rwanda's apocalypse. It is a place where wars, genocides, massacres, persecution, martyrdom, injustice, imprisonment, betrayal, and survival happened.

May the Good Lord give us the strength to endure, compassion toward the oppressed, and understanding to act!

THE APPEAL

There used to be a time when life was regarded as sacred. A time when we believed that no life is without worth or is inconsequential. A time when we all believed that the rights of all people must be defended.

But what has happened? Despite our nation and humanitarian organizations showing us disastrous, alarming human right reports in Rwanda (which get worse year after year), the west has chosen to turn the other way and, instead of defending human lives, has praised the regime for their economic development and miracles instead. This has resulted in a very dangerous situation in Rwanda. This man, who has the power and means to save all Rwandans and let them live in peace has chosen to give them over to slaughter!

What does the West know about Kagame's dreadful human rights abuses and his gruesome reprisal massacres that are happening inside Rwanda daily? What does the world know about Kagame's unrestrained persecution against Christians and his extermination of Hutus and Tutsi critics? Why is the West waiting to denounce this evil?

CURRENT SITUATION

Rwandans, especially Christians, Hutus, and Tutsis critics are being massacred. Rwandans are not allowed to flee the bloody regime. Rwandans are not allowed to travel, except those on Kagame's special list. Rwandans are not allowed to speak up about the wrong being done to them. Rwandans are not allowed to express themselves.

In Rwanda, there is no independent journalism. Journalists are not allowed to report without the government interfering, so all the atrocities go on without being covered by the media. Rwandans' rights have been stripped away. Rwandans are not allowed to protest. When there are massacres, nobody reports it and no Rwandans are allowed to speak about it, nor to flee.

If they cannot speak up, if they cannot protest, if they cannot flee, it seems the only option left for them, if we do not rescue them, is TO DIE HELPLESSLY WHILE THE WORLD IS WATCHING AND DOING NOTHING.

There is also a great famine in Rwanda that the people are not allowed to talk about. There is much more going on that destroys the lives of many. What is happening inside Rwanda does not get out. Only one side of the story is told, so the world is blind and does not question their human rights abuses.

Dear International Community,

You are a great people – the world depends on you. I am asking you to remember that a handcuffed person in prison cannot set themselves free. Please, look at Rwanda with compassion. Put the precious lives of people before development or anything else, and come to rescue Rwandans.

Do not turn a blind eye as you did during the 1994 Genocide. Today is a new day. Today we can do better.

- I am asking you, the most powerful nations on earth, to look at the Rwanda human rights reports by the U.S. State Department, the Human Rights Watch, Amnesty International, and others human rights organizations and think about thousands of people dying inside Rwanda while the world does nothing.
- I am asking you, President Trump, to please do what is in your power to save Rwandans and put an end to the terrorism and genocide they have been suffering through for

the past 30 years. You understand first-hand what injustice is, so please give them the gift of justice.

- Today I am asking you, António Guterres, to confront dictators, to not fear powerful rulers, nor cover up their ugly crime, but to stand up and truly put first the protection of helpless refugees everywhere. I am pleading with you, do not fear the strong and do the job the United Nations should do – protecting refugees and stopping anyone from kidnapping and massacring them. To bring to justice murderers of refugees and the helpless. God stands with you when you do the right thing.

- I am asking you, Boris Johnson. I am appealing to you, please do the right thing for Rwanda. What Rwanda needs first and foremost is not the financial help. What Rwandans are begging for at this time are their lives.

- I am asking you, Benjamin Netanyahu, and all Israel, you, whose ancestors have gone through the Holocaust, to take a look and know what truly happened in the Rwanda genocide. Read the other side of the story. Read my story and act on behalf of all the millions that died through the genocides and massacres at the hand of the Rwanda regime.

- To Vice President Mike Pence, Secretary Mike Pompeo, and Ambassador Sam Brownback, I am asking you, please, to do all that is in your power to protect Christians in Rwanda. Since 2018, the government has become very hostile toward the church. They have destroyed most of the real church and thousands of clergymen. The Kagame regime has secretly killed and imprisoned countless Christians, one family at a time.

- I am asking all lawmakers, senators, and congress men and women to save Rwandans from lobbyists. They are lobbying for a dictator who imprisons and kills anyone he dislikes. They are robbing Rwandans of their lives. Listen to the other side of the story and know the truth.

- I am asking you, the European Union, you who are a powerful body, give Rwandans life before you give them your financial support. Help Rwandans by conducting an independent investigation on the massacre going on inside Rwanda daily.

- I am asking you, my brothers and sisters, leaders of the African continent, to rise up as one and come to uproot evil that is worming its way into our beautiful culture.

- Today I am asking all of you to lay aside the myths you have been told about Rwanda. Don't let the great shining city of Kigali blind you, just as Kagame has planned. I am asking you to look beyond the whitewashed tomb city and to think about the innocent lives perishing inside the city's many safe houses, the city's prisons, and their torture chambers. Think about the lives being destroyed every day, and for the past 30 years! I am inviting you all to make a real investigation into these things I am about to share with you.

May the Almighty God bless you. May He cause truth to triumph!

1

GET TO KNOW THE REAL RWANDA

RWANDA'S 30 YEARS APOCALYPSE BRIEF HISTORY

On October 1, 1990, there was a war against Rwanda by Rwanda Patriotic Front (RPF) who was led by General Major Fred Rwigyema. He was also the founder of the RPF. On the second day of this invasion, Fred was mysteriously killed and was replaced by Paul Kagame.

At the moment of this invasion, I was 18 years old and I remember very well the Rwanda of my childhood–the beautiful land of a thousand hills. Before this invasion, Rwanda and the Great Lakes Region enjoyed peace that ran like a river, long and enduring. From the moment of this invasion onward, however, something new began to take place in Rwanda - killings, kidnapping, raping, bloodshed, and carnage! To us it was a true invasion.

From that day, Rwanda plunged into the darkness of the night. RPF began penetrating Rwandan territories from Uganda, killing civilians along the way and forcing hundreds of thousands of refugees to flee their lands. From that moment to this day Rwanda, the country that once knew peace, would never be the same again.

The president of Rwanda at the time of invasion was Juvenal Habyarimana. Two years after the invasion, desperate to end this war, he sat at the negotiation table with his opponents and signed the Arusha Peace Accords. On the night of April 6, 1994, as president Habyarimana was returning from signing the peace accords with his opponent Kagame, his plane was downed by a missile, killing two presidents aboard, Habyarimana and Cyprien Ntaryamira, the President of Burundi, prominent members of their cabinets, and three French aircraft crew.

It is believed by many experts that the mastermind behind the shutting down of the presidential airplane was none other than Paul Kagame, who was thirsty for power. Those of us who were in Rwanda at the time have no doubt about this. We know who introduced killings to Rwanda. We know who has killed from the beginning.

We also know about the people around him who disappear mysteriously. Kagame's former bodyguards and staff, who dared to come forward and testify about RPF downing this plane, have either been killed or disappeared.

The assassination of President Habyarimana caused rage

among citizens, as Habyarimana was loved by the majority of the population. His assassination, and the assassination of other political figures which followed his death, triggered the Rwanda genocide in which 800,000 people were killed within three months. Following these assassinations, neither party observed the Arusha accords and Kagame moved on with the war. He won in July, 1994. It was then that the genocide against Tutsi stopped, but it did not stop for the Hutus.

From July, 1994, Kagame, who is also from the Tutsi tribe, became the Vice President of Rwanda and at the same time, the Minister of Defense, while Pasteur Bizimungu from the Hutu tribe became the new president.

By 1994, Rwanda's population was about 7 million, comprised of three ethnic groups: Hutu with 85 percent of the population; Tutsi with 14 percent; and the Twa with one percent. In the year 2000, however, Kagame forced president Bizimungu to resign and he became the President of Rwanda, thus the minority reigned over the majority. He has been the president of Rwanda for 20 years now and does not seem to have plans to retire.

From then on there has never been peace, justice, or truth in Rwanda, and this has greatly affected the entire Great Lakes Region. In Rwanda, disappearances and extra judicial killings have become a lifestyle. On a daily basis, unarmed civilians are secretly snatched away, kidnapped, to never be seen again.

Kagame's regime is also hostile towards Christians and oftentimes pastors and Christians are killed, arrested, put in chains, and thrown in jail without justice. Thousands are brutally murdered every year, killed like flies or something that has no value. Every killing is top secret, done with much effort, and lots of money is invested in this so that the international community is clueless of what's truly going on. Every evidence of the killings must be destroyed at all cost, and anyone who witnesses the killings must be killed to conceal everything.

No matter how mysterious they try to make it, no matter their esoteric plan, God, the Supreme Being, always leaves a witness behind. Those who have eyes to see and ears to hear, they will see and hear, but they must search first.

It is shocking to see that not many people in Europe or North America seem to know what is really going on in Rwanda! It is also shocking that most of his supporters are churches and Christians who have no clue that they are joining hands with an antichrist spirit to persecute and martyr their own brothers!

This is why I must tell you about Rwanda's 30 years of apocalypse and the great tribulation – so that nobody can say, "I never knew!" I will present to you the real Rwanda! The Rwanda that most tourists and expatriates have not seen, the Rwanda that the Kagame political propagandists dare not talk about, nor expose to anyone! The real Rwanda, Kagame's empire built for a show. The great city of Kigali, the cleanest in Africa, and according to Rwanda, the cleanest in the whole world!

"The great city", they say. "There is none like it." In reality, it is a manicured grave plot which, if you dare put any effort into it, to dig a little bit, you will find out that a few feet down it is full of the bones of the dead and every form of uncleanliness and abomination.

KAGAME'S LINK TO THE ROYAL FAMILY [1]

In 1896, Kanjogera, a Tutsi queen from the Abega clan, organized a coup against her stepson and legal Tutsi King, Mutara Rutarindwa. This happened after her husband, the great King Kigeli IV Rwabugiri died.

King Rwabugiri was considered one of Rwanda's most powerful kings who conquered many kingdoms and expanded Rwanda territory. He was a man of war and he ruthlessly eliminated possible rivals and purged the leadership of several armies.

Before his death in 1889, King Rwabugiri had proclaimed his son Rutarindwa co-ruler, thereby designating him the successor to his throne. A few years earlier, the king had killed the new king's mother (who was also his wife) by court decree. King Rwabugiri therefore made Kanjogera, his other wife, to be the adoptive queen mother of the newly chosen King Rutarindwa.

On king Rwabugiri's death in 1895, Rutarindwa was proclaimed the new king.

Kanjogera had a son of her own named Musinga and, with the help of two powerful brothers, she orchestrated a palace coup and placed 10-year-old Musinga on the throne instead. Kanjogera and her brothers were effectively in charge at his point, as Musinga was still too young to rule. The two continued to purge rivals who had survived Kigeli IV's purge, as to avoid the possibility that they would return to power.

I spoke to my friend David Himbara, a former advisor to president Kagame and now an author and professor of international development who is in exile in Canada. I asked him if these things were so and he told me this story: "My great grandfather Nzigiye was an adviser to King Rwabugiri. In his work at the court, Nzigiye was always challenging Queen Kanjogera, wife of Rwabugiri. When Rwabugiri and Nzigiye died, Kanjogera and her brothers, Kabare and Ruhinankiko, killed the new King Rutarindwa. They crowned the ten-year-old Musinga as the new king. Because Kanjogera hated the late Nzigiye, he wanted to kill his two sons, Rukizangabo and Rwatangabo. Rukizangabo and Rwatangabo, were my grandfather and his brother. They fled to Ankole until 1930 when Kanjogera died. My father Babyagamba was born in exile in Ankole, in current Uganda. Having returned to Rwanda, in 1960, my father and I fled again during the Hutu revolution to Uganda. I grew up outside Rwanda as a result until I moved to Rwanda in 2000." Himbara fled Rwanda in 2010 to South Africa. He made me laugh when he said, "In my family, we are professional refugees since 1896!"

RELIGIOUS LIFE AT THE COURT

At the court, the king and the queen mother Kanjogera practiced the rites of ancestor worship cults. Kubandwa, Nyabingi, and Ryangombe converged with Rwandan healing practices and witchcraft known as Abacwezi. When the first missionaries came to Rwanda, Kanjogera's court rejected Christianity and believed Christianity should be only for Hutu and Twas tribes. The royal family kept the traditional religion of Abacwezi and participated in these cult practices. It was so important to them that they appointed a resident priest of the cult at the court.

Queen Kanjogera, wife to King Rwabugiri, mother to Umwami Musinga was also aunt to Kagame's father Rutagambwa. In other words, Queen Kanjogera was Kagame's great aunt.

FROM GENOCIDE TO DEMOCIDE

The killings of Rwandans have not stopped just because the '94 Genocide is over. From genocide, Rwanda plunged into democide.

By definition, democide is the willful murder of any person or people by their government. This includes government-sponsored large-scale killings for racial or political reasons. It is very dangerous when the government kills its citizens! It is a fearful thing!

Democide is what has been happening in Rwanda following the genocide of 1994. To this day, the government has unlawful secret detentions, numerous torture chambers, and even kills citizens for their critical viewpoints. This happens daily, and most of the time they go unreported in the mainstream media because the totalitarian president keeps a tight grip on the press.

The massacres against Christians who truly follow the Bible, the people of faith, all freedom fighters, and all lovers, is at an all-time high. Those with critical thinking and views are considered Rwanda enemy and they are disappearing every day by the hand of the government. The international community is unaware of this.

Authoritarianism and censorship are rampant. People are afraid to talk, even in their own homes because they do not know what kind of listening devices might be installed there. So, when they talk private, they prefer to go to a park or somewhere outdoors, leaving behind their phones.

As I write this book, the Rwandan citizens are not allowed to text, email, or say anything negative about the current regime.

Anyone who does it, does it at their own risk. Rwandans are not allowed to express their pains, nor talk about their current sad situation, such as the famine that is ravaging the land. Anyone who does so, and is caught, is considered an enemy. Every day they are in danger of being imprisoned or killed.

IMPRISONMENT IN RWANDA

Imprisonment is a daily threat. Currently, there are more prisons and safe houses in Rwanda than there are clinics or schools. Almost every citizen has received imprisonment threats, and I cannot think of a family in Rwanda that has not had a member put in prison. From the former president and politicians to the common man, they have all spent time in jail, while they have done nothing deserving of imprisonment!

There are thousands of great people—fathers, mothers, and grandparents—who have been in jail since 1994. The sad thing is that they have committed no crime. There are many parents who never got to raise their children because they have been locked up for over 25 years and, among these, many have not committed any crimes. There are many children who were forced to live like orphans and are now in college having never received the tender touch of a mother or a father.

The sad thing is that in many instances, the commander-in-chief is aware of this! He knows there are innocent people who are in jail but because of who they are: ethnicity, relatives of his opponents, those who refuse to join his ruling party RPF, those who seem to be a threat to him in any way, they must languish in Kagame's prisons and to this day he refuses to let them go. To this day he keeps filling those prisons with innocent lives! Recently, a phone conversation between two high-ranking officers leaked in which they were talking how the prisons are so overcrowded, that to make room they have no other choices but to have some people killed. The whole conversation of this telephone call is included in this book.

The citizens of Rwanda are not allowed to travel. The only ones allowed to do so are those who worship Kagame and his regime. Recently, two women who had run against president Kagame were released after being in jail for one year (Diane Rwigara) and for eight years (Victoire Ingabire). The government of Rwanda would not let them travel abroad to speak or receive their awards.

On December 5, 2019, the government of Rwanda barred Victoire Ingabire, the first Rwandan women to run for president against Kagame, from leaving the country to receive the 2019 International Human Rights Award given by the Human Rights Association of Spain (APDHE). "I wrote a letter to the Minister of Justice requesting permission to travel but the minister didn't reply as usual. It's unfortunate," Ingabire told The Associated

Press"

The whole country has become a gigantic prison. Today I am sounding the alarm, asking for the world to come together and set these captives free! The human race is one. What we lift up from others cannot weigh upon us. Helping other to be free gives us all more freedom.

RWANDA'S ATMOSPHERE BEFORE KAGAME'S ARRIVAL

Before his arrival, Rwanda was a little heaven on earth. Where I was born, Hutus and Tutsis played together in harmony. We played under the moon and stars, and sometimes when we went to bed, we would leave our doors unlocked. The sound of a gun was unheard of. No soldiers walked around fully armed, nor was there anyone who lorded it over us with guns. We enjoyed basic human rights.

Before his arrival:

No clergy had ever been killed for their faith by the government.

No citizens were ever killed for their beliefs.

No citizens were ever kidnapped or went missing for days, months, or years.

No refugees nor displaced persons were inside the country.

No guns or weapons were ever heard.

No violence ever against journalists.

We enjoyed freedom of association and peaceful assembly.

Rwanda was a true paradise to everyone.

Jails were sometimes empty, especially in the rural areas! There was no Directorate of Military Intelligence (DMI) nor Rwanda Investigation Bureau (RIB). Both are seen as abductions, targeted killings, and mass killing machines. When you mention DMI/RIB to Rwandan citizens, everyone trembles because they have seen those two agencies be a repository of death, malevolence, and hellish torment.

Before, there used to be truth, love, peace, and trust, and where I lived for 20+ years, there was no censorship whatsoever! It was a country where peace ran like a river. It was said in one of the presidential speeches at the time, and it was heard in some songs:

"Fellow citizens,

God has not chosen to give us diamonds,

God has not chosen to bless us with gold nor precious stones,

But God has chosen to bless us with peace – peace that runs like a river!"

Proof: Read all the human rights reports and the U.S. State Department reports prior to 1990. Also, do your own research. You will find out that there were no kidnappings, no imprisonments, no tortures, no killings, and no wars in the Great Lakes region. No one was ever shot trying to cross into the neighboring countries.

RWANDA ATMOSPHERE AFTER THE INVASION

But one day, things changed overnight without warning!

In October, 1990, Kagame's army invaded Rwanda. Upon his invasion, for the first time, guns were heard in the country. The newcomers came, shedding much blood in territories they occupied, provoking everyone to anger. Little by little, they infiltrated different corners of the country, sometimes sending unsuspected children soldiers throughout the country! At first, killings were reported in territories occupied by RPF, but later on everywhere throughout the country. Killings were done by experts; you could see bodies but not so easily figure out who killed them.

This was definitely a new thing in Rwanda. These killings did not spare anyone! They did not spare the elders, nor the young nor infants. They did not spare the rulers, nor the common man. They did not spare the bride, nor the groom; men and women alike languished throughout the country.

With the coming of Kagame and the RPF, there came great mourning throughout Rwanda. The rich and the poor groaned and the beauty of the colors faded away. Division and suspicion came forth; everything turned black and white.

In the past, I had read that the people of faith were oftentimes respected and spared during the time of war, but not so in

Rwanda. I remember that one day during the genocide, Rwanda religious society suffered a great blow when three bishops, one archbishop, nine priests, and one brother were brutally murdered by Kagame's RPF!

The killings did not just stop there but took the lives of parents, children, and the weak. They were drowned and bodies of people began to float on rivers and lakes throughout Rwanda. The never-seen-before was observed throughout Rwanda. It was like watching a horror movie. From that day forward, Rwanda began her 30 year apocalypse, and now it has gotten worse.

RWANDA ATMOSPHERE RIGHT AFTER GENOCIDE: 10,000 PEOPLE KILLED PER MONTH

After the genocide in 1994, revenge, elimination politics, and injustice ruled Rwanda. A regime full of deception and lies was in place, yet to the outside world they made themselves look blameless!

They destroyed families in many ways. For example, fathers, especially Hutus, and sometimes mothers, were put in jail, even though they were innocent. They were separated from their small children who were under three years old, in many cases to never see them again. They seized peoples' estates, threw people in jail, and would tell a bogus story or use close relatives to testify against people. They would not give the relatives a choice. Either they testified or they disappeared, too. They taught children to report on their parents and vice versa, and they would reward those who reported on others. Rwanda became a world of INJUSTICE, where the regime rewarded lies and fought truth.

Within months of Kagame taking power, a leaked report from the U.S. State Department confirmed that the United Nations High Commissioner for Refugees investigative team spent July and August in Rwanda. They reported systematic killings in the country while Kagame was in charge. The team estimated that Kagame's army and Tutsi civilian surrogates were killing 10,000 or more Hutu civilians per month, with the army accounting for 95 percent of the killings.

Right after the genocide, many non-governmental organizations poured into Rwanda to help rebuild the country. At this time, the presence of the international community was large inside Rwanda. Even that did not slow the pace of the killings by Kagame's army. The killings go on to this day, although the numbers may be less than they had been.

United States Department of State

Washington, D. C. 20520

9/19/94

INFORMATION MEMORANDUM

S/S

DECL: OADR

TO: The Secretary

THROUGH: P - Mr. Tarnoff

FROM: AF - George E. Moose

SUBJECT: New Human Rights Abuses in Rwanda

SUMMARY

A UNHCR investigative team that spent July and August in Rwanda has reported systematic human rights abuses by GOR forces -- including systematic killings -- in the south and southeast of the country. The team has concluded that the GOR is aware of these reprisals against Hutu civilians and may have sanctioned them. A UN delegation now in Kigali will raise this issue with the GOR and ask what steps will be taken to halt the abuse. The UN/UNHCR plan public release of the report this week, and we plan to raise this issue with the GOR in the context of the September 20-23 Wirth visit to Kigali.

DISCUSSION

The September 17 debriefing of members of a UNHCR team that spent July and August in Rwanda revealed that the Rwandan Patriotic Army (RPA), the military wing of the Rwandan Patriotic Front (RPF), has engaged in a pattern of systematic killing of Hutu civilians in the south and southeast of Rwanda. The UNHCR team witnessed Hutu men with arms bound in the company of RPA troops and Tutsi civilians. The soldiers possessed two-way radios and knew the "party-line", indicating that their activities were not unknown to authorities in Kigali.

On the basis of interviews with refugees/individuals, the UNHCR team concluded that a pattern of killing had emerged. The RPA convened meetings of displaced persons to discuss peace and security. Once the displaced persons were assembled, RPA soldiers moved in and killed them. In addition

97D241 •1879

to these massacres, the RPA engaged in house to house sweeps and hunted down individuals hiding in swamps. Victims were usually killed with hoes, axes, machetes and fire. Although males aged 18-40 were at highest risk, the young and elderly were not spared. The team estimated that the RPA and Tutsi civilian surrogates had killed 10,000 or more Hutu civilians per month, with the RPA accounting for 95% of the killing.

The UNHCR team speculated that the purpose of the killing was a campaign of ethnic cleansing intended to clear certain areas in the south of Rwanda for Tutsi habitation. The killings also served to reduce the population of Hutu males and discouraged refugees from returning to claim their lands.

The UNHCR team informed us that they will raise their finding with GOR Defence Minister Paul Kagame in Kigali, possibly by September 21. They will inquire of Kagame what steps he will take to stop the killings. UNSYG Boutros Ghali plans to brief the Security Council and subsequently make the gist of the UNHCR report public. We have been asked not to get out in front of the UN on this issue to avoid putting individuals and NGOs at risk.

We intend to take complementary action. We will use Under Secretary Wirth's September 22-23 meetings with Kagame and other senior GOR officials to raise this issue and to underline U.S. commitment to respect human rights and the rule of law if the UN has made its demarche. We will report further on this issue following the GOR response.

This document details what our beloved friends and families who were left behind after the genocide experienced. Those who escaped these massacres told us exactly the same.

This document states,

"The September 17 debriefing of members of a UNHCR team that spent July and August in Rwanda revealed that the Rwandan Patriotic Army (RPA), the military wing of the Rwandan Patriotic Front (RPF), has engaged in a pattern of systematic killing of Hutu civilians in the South and Southeast of Rwanda. The UNHCR team witnessed Hutu men with arms bound in the company of RPA troops and Tutsi civilians. The soldiers possessed two-way radios and knew the "party-line", indicating that their activities were not unknown to authorities in Kigali.

On the basis of interview with refugees/individuals, the UNHCR team concluded that a pattern of killing had emerged. The RPA convened meetings of displaced person to discuss peace and security. Once the displaced persons were assembled, RPA soldiers moved in and killed them. In addition to these massacres, the RPA engaged in house to house sweeps and hunted down individuals hiding in swamps. Victims were usually killed with hoes, axes, machetes and fire. Although males aged 18-40 were at highest risk, the young and elderly were not spared. The team estimated that the RPA and Tutsi civilian surrogates had killed 10,000 or more Hutu civilians per month, with the RPA accounting for 95 percent of the killing."

Judi Rever is an investigative journalist and international speaker. In 2018, she wrote a book *"In Praise of Blood: The crimes of the Rwandan Patriotic Front."* [2] It is the book that that I found best described what took place in Rwanda during the time of war and the genocide. It is the most genuine book, and the one best described what I experienced in Rwanda.

The summary says that in this book, Rever conducted hundreds of interviews "with RPF defectors, former soldiers, and atrocity survivors. Supported by documents leaked from a U.N. court, Judi Rever brings us the complete history of the Rwandan genocide. Considered by the international community to be the saviors who ended the Hutu slaughter of innocent Tutsis, Kagame and his rebel forces were also killing, in quiet and in the dark, as ruthlessly as the Hutu genocidaire were killing in daylight. The reason why the larger world community hasn't recognized this truth? Kagame and his top commanders effectively covered their tracks and, post-genocide, rallied world guilt and played the heroes in order to attract funds to rebuild Rwanda, and to maintain and extend the Tutsi sphere of influence in the region."[3] This book is heartbreaking, chilling, and necessary. I recommend it to everyone.

Those who committed such atrocities instead of being brought to justice are the ones who lead the country. They are the ones who gave the narrative of what took place. They are the ones who investigated the killings and brought forth justice! This is why to this day, the killings, the tortures, and injustice have not stopped inside Rwanda. Rwanda has a serious problem. They could not give what they do not have. Those who kill cannot give life. Those who do injustice cannot give justice. All the world, please come to the rescue of Rwandans.

2

CHRISTIAN PERSECUTION & MARTYRDOM

THE CASE OF KIZITO MIHIGO

30 Years After RPF Invasion, Rwanda's Apocalypse Continues

Never before in my life had I seen such a saint, a true worshiper who leads worshipers into the third dimension and into the presence of God. He is a man full of love, compassion, and forgiveness to all. His name is Kizito Mihigo.

On February 17, 2020, Rwanda police announced that Mihigo was found dead in his cell at Remera Police Station in Kigali, having committed suicide.

Mihigo was a musical child prodigy and he grew up to be the most prominent artist Rwanda had, a rare musician, a singer, songwriter, organist, and composer of sacred music. In short, the Mozart of Africa. He was the composer of Rwanda's national anthem. He was also a television presenter, a 1994 genocide survivor, and an apostle of love, peace, and reconciliation.

Rwandan gospel singer and the most prominent artist Kizito Mihigo was found dead in police custody on February 17, 2020. #JusticeForKizito

"If You Don't Do What Kagame Says, You Will Be a Dead Man"

In March, 2014, Mihigo released a song of reconciliation titled 'Igisobanuro cy'Urupfu' – 'The Meaning of Death.' It was a message of reconciliation, of unity, and love to remember all that died during the genocide, including Hutus. Kagame did not like the song and instead he turned against Mihigo and had him imprisoned and tortured. While in prison, Mihigo confided to some friends that he believed he would be killed; therefore, he made some recordings while in prison and sent them to a human rights activist abroad, asking that they should only be released should he be assassinated.

On February 21, 2020, Channel TV 4 in the U.K. received that recording and released it.

"After the release of the song, I received insults, threats, and messages saying that something bad would happen to me," Mihigo said. "I was invited for an interview with Rwanda President's Chief of Staff, Ines Mpambara, which took place in the office of the senate president, who was at the time the senate vice president. Both of them spoke to me and said, "The president didn't like my song and I should write a letter asking for pardon. Ines Mpambara and the senate vice president said that if I didn't do what they said, I was a dead man!"

Did He Change Overnight

How can this be? A man who once was like a son to the president, who at one time lived with the first family, and who served the president faithfully; a man who once traveled with the presidential team singing the national anthem, and who served his country selflessly – how can he be rewarded with murder? How can it be that Mihigo, who once received the First Lady of Rwanda's award in recognition of his artistic activities for peace and reconciliation, all of sudden be arrested on suspicion of plotting terrorist attacks against the country and the president he loved? How can it be that he who chose to fully consecrate his life and his work to forgiveness and reconciliation in Rwanda be called a terrorist? Did he change overnight?

After spending 10 years mastering music in Europe, though he was given an opportunity to stay through Belgian parents who had adopted him, though there were many opportunities for him to become very famous abroad, he chose to give it up all for the love of his country, Rwanda.

Kizito Mihigo's Life[1]

On July 25, 1981, one year before the apparitions of Virgin Mary in Kibeho, a baby boy was born in the small town of Gikongoro to Augustin Buguzi who was the school headmaster and Placidie Ilibagiza, a teacher at the same primary school.
The devout catholic couple called him Kizito, the name of one of the Uganda martyrs, and Mihigo, the name of his grandfather. Kizito was the third child of a family that would grow to have six children.

Mihigo's passion for music was revealed at a very young age. Before he was even 10 years old, he was already writing and composing religious songs to the delight of his family and parish. When the Rwanda war started in 1990, Mihigo was 9 years old and completely clueless about what was going on. All that he remembered was his father spending more time at the church praying for the welfare of his country.

In April, 1994, when the genocide started, his father sent his wife and kids to a neighboring parish, Karama in Runyinya commune. Mihigo's father stayed behind as his elderly mother could not make the journey.

Their stay in Karama was nightmarish. There were constant attacks against those who took refuge there and bodies were piling up all around the room where they were hiding. After a couple of weeks, they were separated during a violent assault. Mihigo walked with the crowds, fleeing to Burundi, not knowing if he would ever see his family again. Mihigo was miraculously reunited with his mother and siblings in the weeks that followed his arrival in Burundi.

After the genocide, the family went back and found out his father did not make it. He died during the Rwanda genocide. Mihigo was filled with rage and was intent on avenging his father. He tried to join the new army as a child soldier but his uncle admonished him, and he was enrolled back in school.

After completing his primary school in 1995, Mihigo joined the seminary, Virgo Fidelis of Karubanda in Butare, not so much to become a priest but because of a promise he had made to his late father.

In Karubanda, Mihigo found refuge in karate, music, and prayer. His rage and hatred dissipated. The 14-year-old Mihigo composed dozens of liturgical songs that were soon played in all the Catholic churches in the country. In his second year, he created a choir and by the time he was 19, he had written more than 200 original songs in the most beautiful and purest of Kinyarwanda.

In 2001, after participating in a competition to compose the country's new national anthem, 19 year old Mihigo was offered a scholarship to study at music academy Court Saint Etienne in Belgium for a year, and the renowned Music Conservatory of Paris from which he graduated in 2008.

In 2010, he created the Kizito Mihigo Peace Foundation, a non-profit foundation with the objective to use Art for Peace, Reconciliation, Unity, Nonviolence and Human Dignity in Rwandan society after the 1994 genocide. When he returned to Rwanda in 2011, he toured schools and prisons to talk about reconciliation.

In 2012, Mihigo started broadcasting a weekly television program called Umusanzu w'Umuhanzi, 'The Artist's Contribution,' in which people of different faith discussed about peacebuilding, forgiveness, and reconciliation. In 2009, his song Twanze Gutoberwa Amateka, "Don't Weaponize our History," in which he denounced the misuse of the genocide and history's tragedies to separate Rwandans became an instant hit, making him one of the country's most prominent artists.

In recognition of his activities for peace, Mihigo was awarded the Celebrating Young Rwandan Achievers by the Imbuto foundation, an organization of Jeannette Kagame Nyiramongi, the wife of General Kagame. The Rwanda Governance Board recognized the Kizito Mihigo Peace Foundation among the top-ten local NGOs that had promoted good governance in Rwanda. He became the darling of the first family but not for too long. His heart was set on his Christian faith to live righteously and inclusively. A life of love and true forgiveness.

His messages were, unfortunately, not to the liking of Kagame and those around him who had begun weaponizing genocide and profiteering from it. 'Igisobanuro cy'Urupfu,' 'The Meaning of Death' in which he boldly shows compassion for both the victims of the genocide of Hutus and the victims of revenge killings and their families, did not please Kagame. The song was banned by Kagame across Rwanda in the hours that followed its release in March, 2014.

The Song that Cost A Man's Life

This was the song that made him Kagame's public enemy. A song that would later cost him his life. What's in it that is worthy of a death sentence?

The Meaning of Life

There is no worst thing than death
But what a path for us
A path for us, a path to good, the greater good

Death is the door, that leads to God, the Creator
But in order to get that door open
The summoning voice of God is required
In Kinyarwanda it is said,
Dying is to respond to God's summon

Nothing such as a good death
Be it by genocide or war
Be it by slaughter in revenge
Vanished in an accident or by illness
Those loved ones, where they are seated are praying for us

Even though genocide orphaned me
But let it not make me lose empathy for others
Their lives too, were brutally taken
Even though not qualified as genocide

Those brethren,
They too are humans and I pray for them
They too are humans I comfort them
They too are humans I remember them

My dignity and love

Is not rooted in carnal life
Nor in material possessions
But in humanness
Let not Ndi Umunyarwanda (I am Rwandan) come before "I
am human"

The understanding of my salvation
Is my staff of life journey
I was saved by faith
Faith I have in Jesus Christ
That Christianity fulfills me as Rwandan

Death joins people to God
Who created them
And they live in the Agape love of the Father
That love
Is my thirst that my life longs for

That love
Is the hope of eternal life
That love
Is the direction to eternal life
Amen!

The Song Exposed Ethnic Differentiation and the

Commercialization of Genocide

According to observers and analysts, the message of the song, which puts Tutsi and Hutu victims on an equal footing, offended those who would not forgive fully and it provoked the rage of the Rwandan president and his regime, which has institutionalized ethnic differentiation and the commercialization of the Rwandan tragedy of 1994.

A week after this song was released, Mihigo, the beloved artist, mysteriously disappeared from the public without being given a chance to say a word to his fans. He reappeared a week after the commemoration of the genocide that claimed his father's life, was handcuffed, and in police custody.

On February 21, 2020, Benedict Moran of PBS News Hour released an excerpt from an interview with Kizito Mihigo, done in secret while he was imprisoned in 2018. "Rwanda is an open-air prison...If you bring up the subject of other victims, people who were killed by the RPF, you're labeled a genocide denier, or a revisionist." Mihigo said.

"In 2014, I wasn't just arrested, I was abducted and detained for a long time. I was told that I had to plead guilty. They said if I didn't plead guilty, they would kill me. My imprisonment had two reasons. There is a real, hidden reason. And that's the song I released in March, 2014. The song was about reconciliation. I got to a point where I felt compassion for all victims. Not just victims of the genocide against the Tutsi, of which I am one, but also victims of other violence committed by the ruling RPF. Even war crimes and crimes against humanity, but I couldn't help myself."

Mihigo Torture for Seven Days

Mihigo confided to his friends that during the week when everybody thought he disappeared, he was held in incommunicado, being tortured severely. He has told his closest friends that he wrote down all the tortures he endured at the hand of RPF. Some of the tortures included being taken to the cemetery in the night and being terrorized with death. Another time, they took him to a funeral home and showed him the human cremator machine and told him if he does not confess guilty on all accounts, they would grind him in the machine. Mihigo has written of these things in a book that will be released soon by some of his friends.

10 Years in Prison Because President Does Not Like the Song

Mihigo was shown to the journalists before appearing to the prosecution where he pleaded guilty to all fake charges, including the attempted attack on state security, which were fabricated stories. Rwanda government tortures people so mercilessly that the victims have no other option except to accept all the charges.

He was thus condemned to 10 years in Magerere, an infamous prison, on charges of fabricated stories!

When the government of Rwanda comes after you, they make citizens hate you. Using *Rushyashya*, which is Kagame's Propaganda machine newspaper of deception, they assassinated Mihigo's character and incited many Rwandans to dislike the man whom they loved. They banned his music and harassed his family. In all of this, Mihigo did not retaliate nor say a bad word against anyone.

In prison, he was told to continue asking for forgiveness and if he tells of any of the abuse, he would get a life sentence and die in prison. He lived his incarceration peacefully because, having previously conducted a vast program of education in truth, forgiveness, and reconciliation in all the prisons of Rwanda, he walked the talk. He was also welcomed in the prisons where he preached like a hero. Through the pressure of international community, Kagame pardoned Mihigo on September 15, 2018. Among the 2,000 other prisoners liberated that day was Rwanda's opposition leader, Victoire Ingabire, who had spent eight years behind the bars after an equally spectacular trial.

From the Small Prison to the Gigantic Prison

The whole country of Rwanda has become a gigantic prison. When Mihigo, Rwigara, Ingabire, and others prisoners were released, they were told they could not travel abroad, even within the country they were not allowed to go anywhere, nor get benefits like Rwanda citizens.

When the Kagame regime notices you are not fully on their side, they single you out and they find ways to dismantle and uproot you. From the time of his release, singer Kizito Mihigo wasn't allowed to have a national identity card or a passport. Since September, 2019, local officials, on different occasions, refused to grant him a national identity card citing orders from above. In Rwanda, you can't obtain a passport without a national identity card. Without a national identity, it was impossible for him to access any services, including applying for employment or starting a business. Though Mihigo was being denied his basic human rights, he loved and endured to the end.

While in prison, he had written several music pieces and expected to produce them once free. Unfortunately, once released through presidential grace he realized he was still in prison, though he no longer wore shackles. He was followed, and every movement he made was tracked. His private phone conversations were being listened to. He moved from one studio to another, asking for a chance to record his newly written music, and all studios refused citing orders from above. This is why, since being released on September 15, 2018, he hadn't released any song.

From the time he was released, Mihigo never uttered a

word about the case that cost him four years of his freedom on fabricated charges. Instead, he continued to conduct choirs, teach music to children, and continued to create new songs. In the last three decades, he had composed more than 400 songs purely enshrined in his catholic faith and genuine love for all his fellow Rwandans.

Mihigo's Assassination

On Friday, February 14, 2020, RIB, known to many Rwandans as the Rwanda killing machine, published a press release that it had arrested Mihigo during an attempt to flee to Burundi.

Mihigo mysteriously died on February 17, 2020 while in police custody, with Rwandan authorities immediately attributing the death to suicide. His family confirmed that they were called by the police telling them Mihigo committed suicide by hanging himself, using bedsheets and that his body was found inside the cell prison.

This narrative was disputed by many in the international community. For example, USA Assistant Secretary of State, Tibor Nagy, Fondered how the Rwanda government concluded that Mihigo committed suicide before an inquiry or autopsy was conducted. Secretary Nagy called for an investigation of the circumstances of Mihigo's death. Commonwealth, Human Rights

Watch, and Amnesty International demanded an independent fair investigation but Rwanda refused, saying they are a sovereign nation, would not allow an independent investigation. But if it is the government that has committed the assassination, should they be the ones to investigate themselves?

It was reported that his body was heavily guarded by Rwanda law enforcement. No one was allowed to take a picture. His family was denied the right to clean and dress his remains. On the day of his memorial when it was viewed, no cameras were allowed in the room. A journalist from Ishema TV by the name of Hassan Cyuma Deodone who viewed the body narrated that Mihigo's face had three injuries — on the forehead, on the left and on right cheek. Also, the report made by the RIB spokesperson and Mihigo's lawyer, Me Antoinette Mukamusoni, who is appointed by the government, contradicted each other. Was it truly a suicide or was it the fulfillment of the warning: "Ines Mpambara and the senate vice president said that if I didn't do what they said, I was a dead man!"

Mihigo's Memorial Service and the Funeral

Besides the announcement of his death by the police, there was no government representative that came to Mihigo's farewell ceremonies. There were no condolences; only silence from Kagame regime. "Mr. Mihigo had been a cultural icon in

Rwanda – a hugely popular celebrity and peace activist who often sang the national anthem at state functions," says Geoffrey York, Africa correspondent for The Globe and Mail (Canada). The silence from Kagame and the government on the death of such a celebrity and the composer of the national anthem confirmed to many what they already knew: that the government was involved in Mihigo's death. During that sad moment, the government organized conferences and some Rwanda concerts abroad. It was as if Rwandans were not allowed to mourn the man who was one of the most loved in the country.

This Mihigo case is one of thousands of cases which shows how the Kagame regime has treated Human Rights Defenders for the past 30 years. If someone can murder Mihigo, they are after all freedom fighters, after us all. All the world, we ask you, do not delay. Help us get justice for Mihigo. Thousands upon thousands of "Mihigos" have found death this way. Thousands of more "Mihigos" inside Rwanda will die if the world does not act.

One of Mihigo Last Messages Via a Friend

The conversation below was sent to me by a friend of Mihigo who lives in France and wants to remain anonymous. She testified to talking to Mihigo before he died. She felt that inside their conversations there was a message Mihigo left to all Rwandans.

The friend testified that beyond what human eyes could

see, even behind the scenes, Mihigo was always a man of action. "There is no doubt we have seen his external works and we are thankful for that, but there were also his unseen works," Mihigo friend said.

'The Ongoing Killings of Rwandans Hurt Me So Much'.

"It was on August 29, 2019, when I first talked to Mihigo. He called me and we talked for a short while. He said that he had some important things to share with me," the friend recalls. "Remembering all the victims who died, all the people who are oppressed and suffering from injustice is something I have on my heart. Please forgive me, I am in Rwanda where I am helpless to help anyone. But keep fighting for the truth," Mihigo confided to the friend. "We kept talking about normal things in life for about one month." On September 24, 2019, Mihigo wrote, saying, "The ongoing killings of Rwandans hurt me so much. I do not know what to do!"

Let there Be Justice for Hutus and Tutsis, Let There Be Justice for All

Mihigo friend from France continues to testify, "On October 26, 2019, we talked again. At the time, there was a new article, which talked about the genocide against innocent Hutus. There was an excerpt that Mihigo had shared with me which said, "No matter what happens, I can't deny the massacres that took place against Hutus, whether in Rwanda or in the Congo. But if we should be real, let's say that justice for the Hutus is now impossible." He sent me the excerpt and he shared his opinion saying, "I do not agree at all with this. Even those innocent Hutus should receive due justice. We should do our best and strive for it." That day, we talked about justice, that anyone who is victimized, no matter the race, they should receive due justice. We even shared some ideas on how to answer that article. Per agreement, I responded on his behalf, even though I added some of my thoughts. It was on Mihigo's heart, that even though he was forbidden to talk about this issue, even though his tongues was tied, maybe someone should speak on his behalf and convey the message: "even those non-Tutsi victims should also receive justice."

"Another time when we talked about important things, Mihigo brought up the subject on how people in Europe thought that he forgot them after being released from prison. There are some people who asked him whether he might have forgotten the Hutus after his release. Others thought that he must have abandoned his belief altogether to satisfy the system of the regime," Said Mihigo friend who lives in France.

Rwanda Has Become a Hell

"After we talked, Mihigo responded, 'Prison did not change my firm conviction, nor can it change someone's belief. My convictions before going to jail are the same as after the release.' But he explained to me that after being released from jail, there are things the regime commanded him to not do. 'They forbade me to never again get involved myself with anything that has to do with peace and reconciliation. You are lucky to be released from jail alive. Next time, we will kill you,' they told him. In our conversation, Mihigo added that one thing he had strongly on his heart was the reconciliation of all Rwandans. The other thing he said that moved me and stayed on my heart was a word he used when I told him that if possible, I would love to go to Rwanda for a visit. He told me, 'The strong desire you have to visit Rwanda is the same strong desire I have to get out.' He added, 'Rwanda has become a hell !'" Concludes Mihigo friend from France.

THE CASE OF PASTOR DAVID RUGWIZA AND THE DESTRUCTION OF HIS CHURCH

To protect individuals, names and locations in this story have been slightly changed but the story remains true.

We are in 2019. It has been 22 years since I left Rwanda to migrate to the USA. All that I had seen in Rwanda caused me to encounter and trust the unseen Almighty God. Upon immigrating to the

US, God blessed me beyond words. I work hard and honor God, so He blessed me to live the American dream.

I finished school, married the most handsome man on earth, and the father of my son Christian. I focused on serving God and raising my family, when all of sudden in 2017, two best friends were used by God to wake me to the remembrance of the excessive suffering of Rwandans. One of them, a best friend I will never forget, Sophia Iradukunda whom I had not seen since I left Rwanda.

Iradukunda contacted me out of great concern. She had become a Christian and was a Sunday school teacher in Rwanda. In 2018, Rwanda had begun persecuting Christians, but cunningly so that the outside world is clueless. They had been cracking down on churches but especially the ones that have discernment, imprisoning pastors left and right. In the midst of this persecution, Iradukunda fled to Uganda. She talked to me from Uganda, saying she had not received refugee status yet but was in the process.

"Persecution of Christians and the people of good will is real in Rwanda," she said. Upon hearing this, I did my own research and talked to people on the ground. Indeed, in 2018 alone, within six months' span, Rwanda had closed over 8,000 churches. On top of this, the freedom of speech, press, and assembly went down the hill. People were not even allowed to assemble in parks or forests or caves to hold a Bible study without government permission. "How come this persecution is not being talked about in the news?" I asked myself.

The first thing Kagame did was to destroy independent journalism so that the west, which gives him a lot of aid, will not know the truth. Any journalist whose views were opposed to Kagame's were either silenced through threats, jailed, exiled, or killed. Currently, no journalist is allowed to report on any special event without the story being read and approved by the government's board. In some cases, to report on special events, the government board prepared the story and write it, and the role of the journalist was to just copy and paste. Often times, journalists need permission to even take a picture. True journalists are silenced or threatened. Because of this, much happens inside the country without being reported. The killings, the kidnappings, the tortures, injustice … they all go on without the outside world knowing anything about it.

When the Rwanda government began persecuting Christians, Iradukunda was punished for refusing to praise Kagame regime. "The government has begun to tightly control churches, and many people are being imprisoned and even killed for what they preach," she testified.

Iradukunda was imprisoned three times for refusing to offer praises to the president of Rwanda. "When you preach or teach, if you praise Jesus five times, you should make sure that at least three times, you acknowledge what great things Kagame has done for Rwanda," Iradukunda said to me. She knew that praises only belonged to God. Though they imprisoned her many times, God delivered her.

Iradukunda Survived Poisoning Three Times

Iradukunda kept leading a normal, quiet life but she would not keep quiet when she needed to let the truth out. When the government agents and informants – who are everywhere in the country – suspect that you have complaints about the government, whether true or not, your life is in grave danger. Iradukunda was treated as an enemy and according to the RPF all enemies must die.

So, it was decided that Iradukunda should be eliminated. She was poisoned three times by Rwanda death squads but a miracle happened, and poison could not kill her. God miraculously spared her life from prisons and poison. The last time Iradukunda was in prison for her faith was in the beginning of 2019. From Uganda where she was living, Iradukunda was abducted by Rwanda forces and taken back to Rwanda. For two months, Iradukunda was imprisoned. Before the closure of the Rwanda and Uganda border, it had become a common practice for Rwanda forces to abduct refugees in Uganda and force them back to Rwanda. Once back in Rwanda, she was put in prison for two months.

In prison, Iradukunda was made to sleep on a bare cement floor, without a blanket, and was fed sparingly. She was miraculously released from jail, but her stomach was severely damaged and she required immediate surgery. During this time, she was far from home and family. When the government hunts you down, they isolate you by using fear on any family members or friends who dare to associate with you.

A pastor named David Rugwiza, a righteous man of God and his congregation gathered their courage, took her in as their own daughter, and stood with her to the very end.

The Killings of Pastor Rugwiza and Destruction of His Church

During spring, 2019, I met pastor Rugwiza through Iradukunda. For 2 days, Iradukunda was in a coma due to her stomach surgery. During this time, pastor Rugwiza kept her phone and responded on her behalf. Pastor Rugwiza was a great pastor, a noble man full of wisdom and love towards his flock and country.

The texts we exchanged are a true treasure that I will forever cherish. He was aware of many wicked things the government of Rwanda was doing against the citizens but he tried to stay positive, hoping for the best. Even though he could not talk to me about it openly, I could sense the oppression he was going through like every other Rwandan.

One of his texts read, "Holy greetings! Before Iradukunda's surgery, she asked me to thank you for all the loving-kindness you have shown to her. I have her phone now because she slipped into a coma after surgery. She is not doing too well, and they might transfer her to a bigger hospital. Please pray."

The condition of Iradukunda kept deteriorating. Pastor Rugwiza sent me another message saying, "Please join us in agreement, we are all praying to God, reminding Him the good deeds Iradukunda has done including leading worship, teaching, and how she left her career to serve God and worked for the cause of the orphans, the widows, and the helpless".

He added that before this surgery, Iradukunda stood on this word of God:

"Arise, shine; for your light has come,
And the glory of the LORD has risen upon you.
For behold, darkness will cover the earth
And deep darkness the peoples;
But the LORD will rise upon you
And His glory will appear upon you."
(Isaiah 61:1-2)

There was no other way to save Iradukunda's life, unless I stepped in by sending the money they needed for medical and food in Rwanda. Rwanda boasts of having the best healthcare system in the world but it is all fake. Pastor Rugwiza sent an SOS message saying that since Iradukunda had no health insurance, $270 was required for her to be admitted to the nearest hospital.

"The cost to keep her on oxygen would be $215 per hour, which is required before they give it to anyone. Please help us, Pastor Christine, so that we can save the life of this dear one," he texted me via Iradukunda's phone.

Where does someone who is just released from prison get that kind of money? Many people are in and out of prison, they are being threatened, and they are being hunted down ? How are they to get the money? This is where I responded and felt it was my responsibility to take care of my best friend. Hunger was a killer in Rwanda at that time. I would send $300 for Iradukunda and it would be gone within two weeks because the cost of living has become so expensive.

Rugwiza and Iradukunda confided to me that most people where they live ate only once a day. The cost of medication was beyond understanding and the cost for food was three times what I spend here in US. How did Rwanda get to this place? The famine was ravaging the country so severely that people took turns eating and not many could afford to have two meals a day. How can

Kagame be one of the riches presidents in Africa with a country suffering like this, and you hear nothing about this famine in the news?

Maybe if they sound the alarm, they could receive help. All you would read in Rwanda advertisements were things like: "Rwanda is the ninth safest country on the globe!" "Ninth most transparent government!" "Second most competitive economy in Africa!" The difference between what people on the ground said and what was being advertised about Rwanda was like that of day and night!

Besides the high price to spend the night in the hospital, the cost per shot was $21 dollars; IV was $15 dollars per hour, and one kilogram of sugar was about $3 dollars. Fruit such as tamarillo was selling for $18 per kilogram."

Pastor Rugwiza kept me updated on the progress of Iradukunda. She was to be operated on in three areas due to an ulcer. The surgery had to be redone because the first one was done by someone who did not know what they were doing. Pastor Rugwiza took care of Iradukunda selflessly. He had one milking cow that he dedicated to providing for Iradukunda's basic needs. By selling the milk, he was able to raise some of the money to help, and I also helped her.

When Iradukunda was recovering, the hospital bill was huge. While she was waiting for the money to come in, a racist doctor threatened that he was not afraid to kill her. At that moment, I learned that inside Rwanda, there is also a department established within the official death squad that kills people using nurses and doctors.

"My beloved pastor, we are fighting a great warfare here. In Rwanda things are not what they seem to be in the world news. Hunger is ravaging the country, life is very costly, and there are no jobs for the youth and our church members! But we do not lose heart because we have God who has been with us all these years," he added. Those were among the last words I exchanged with Rugwiza.

Pastor Rugwiza is Killed

June 20, 2019: Then came the fateful day, the day that Rwanda government death squads destroyed pastor Rugwiza in a fake, staged accident. In 2018, when Rwanda began cracking down on churches, within six months the government closed over 8,000 churches and jailed many pastors and bishops. Other pastors and Christians were killed also.

The closing of the churches was justified by the government, saying that churches were built poorly, that they were not safe, that they needed to meet this and that requirement. The churches were closed against the will of the congregation members and pastors. All the churches that the government could not control were candidates to be closed. The churches that let the government control them, tell them what to preach or not, are not persecuted.

Pastor Vincent knew all of that, but he chose to not compromise. In the midst of taking care of his flock and Iradukunda, he stood in truth and he ministered to both Hutus and Tutsis equally. Because of not bending to the government's wishes, they had sought to kill him, but he was blameless and lived carefully so it was hard for them to catch him in any trespasses.

The government of Rwanda has practiced serious killings for as long as I have known them, but as much as possible it was kept top secret. Killing people in their homes is hard and it makes a loud noise, so they came up with new creative ways of killing people in the most terrible horrible ways: staging fake accidents, ambushing cars, and eliminating the victims by hit and run seemed to be the best way to kill many in 2019. Thousands have died this way. After all, it is hard to come up with proof of who killed them when it is a hit and run!

On June 20, 2019, Pastor Rugwiza, together with his team, went out to minister. They were seven people in a two car convoy of a truck and an SUV. The government of Rwanda has means to censor and monitor almost everyone in the country, just like China does. They use the MTN phone company, and instead of serving citizens and keeping privacy, it has become a weapon to spy on citizens.

Pastor Rugwiza did not know that he was being tracked down. He left with his team and they fell into an ambush in the western part of Rwanda. The heavy trucks made to destroy lives smashed into pastor Rugwiza's car and another truck that was part of his convoy, killing all 7 people on board and taking off. As you can see from both cars [accident photos included in this chapter], this is not just an accident. They hit you left and right, side to side; top to bottom! I was told that this is the system the Kagame death squad uses to kill people. There are several pictures like these from Rwanda when people have been killed this way, and the government does not like to see them on internet, so wherever they find them, they do all they can to remove them.

When pictures of such terrible accidents began to surface on the internet and social medias, Kagame's goons got mad. They attacked me and anyone who would dare post them on internet. They even threatened me, telling me to take them down. It shows the wickedness of man, and they did not want to be exposed. I took those pictures down not for their sake but for the sake of those whose families were involved. They even attacked family and friends we have in Rwanda.

They do not like to see their evil deeds being exposed. "*For everyone who does evil hates the Light and does not come to the Light for fear that his deeds will be expose,.*" it says in John 3:20.

I was threatened even when I only posted one picture I received from my friend on the ground.

But these types of pictures kept surfacing on internet. They would be taken by the victims in Rwanda and sent all over by WhatsApp and social media. Then the government's special department of deception came up with an idea to dismiss them. Within hours of their appearance, they would photoshop them, put an old date and insert them in what looked like an old newspaper. They would use the newspaper to refute them. They kept doing this but what they did not know was that the original pictures had none of that.

"And anyone with half a brain will recognize that their edited versions with precise locations, dates, etc., come as immediate responses from your DMI toolbox. It's amazing how your side just happens to have a collection of such incidents from other countries ready to go, isn't it?" One of the people responded on social media. They could not respond to that!

The government of Rwanda has spent fortunes on their department of deception. It is one of the deadly weapons they use to deceive the world, and to destroy many lives. Wherever they see anyone posting those pictures that show their evil deeds on internet, they get mad and make you a target as well.

Iradukunda, still recovering, took a motorcycle to the hospital where pastor Rugwiza was rushed. His body was in shambles. When he got there, there was a little breath left in him. She was by his side before his death. Pastor Rugwiza gathered all his energy and whispered to her, "I have become your sacrifice, I died in your place. My beloved daughter, this is not an accident, but a well-organized, systematic killing. My daughter, I ask you and I know you will do it, go proclaim everywhere the goodness of God. Share what He has done for you, the testimony of how He delivered you from poison and prisons. Go, proclaim it to the end of the earth. The Lord is with you." And then pastor Rugwiza died. Iradukunda's life was devastated. This was a bitter truth to swallow. She could have died too but because of the surgery, she was still recovering, unable to go anywhere with this team!

It Was a Very Sad Moment

The government offices were contacted but they would not conduct any investigation. They also refused to offer any help to bury pastor Rugwiza and said just wrap the body in a blanket and throw it in a common grave. When someone is killed like this, even neighbors are afraid to come to offer help because they are afraid the government would go after them. During the funeral, government spies are sent to listen to the speech and find out if there is anyone who were present at the site where the killings occurred. Anyone who knows must die. People were afraid to help and bury the dead but great pastors from neighboring

SOS - RWANDA'S 30-YEAR APOCALYPSE

countries, mighty men of God who worked with him in the Great Lakes Region, crossed over and buried pastor Rugwiza, this great mighty warrior, in honor!

Staged accidents during the year 2019-2020 took the lives of many Christians, Hutus and Tutsi critics. Vehicles would be hit left and right, side to side, top to bottom. In some cases, death squad agents would come on the scene to finish those who survived. Such was the case of businessman Assinapol Rwigara. Top: Pastor David Rugwiza. Bottom left: Accident that killed pastor Kimenyi.

LEAVE NOBODY TO TELL

According to RPF philosophy, after the elimination of the target, the family and their business (if they have one) must be crippled, destroyed, or scattered so that nobody grow strong enough to think about revenge. Nobody should be left to tell stories of what happened.

After Pastor Rugwiza's death, his wife was given a 14 days' notice to move out or she would be evicted. They were a poor congregation that had a big heart to help people. Pastor Rugwiza left behind a wife and three children, and within a short time they become homeless, wandering around hungry and afflicted.

Elimination of Pastor Rugwiza's Child

On Sunday July 21, 2019, more sad news came for Rugwiza's family. The same system that took the life of Rugwiza took the life of his child. This child was very smart in school, always recognized as the most brilliant child while the children of their enemies had bad grades.

The child had gone to fetch water and never came back. Later on, a body was found in Nyabarongo River. People who were close to this family testified that this is the same method often used by the death squad team to drown children. Why? Because they know the opposition of Rwanda's government are offspring of those whom Kagame killed or abused. Now, their new way of doing things is to wipe out entire households. Leave nobody to tell!

Elimination of Pastor Rugwiza's Wife and Another Child

On August 4, 2019, another staged accident took place to destroy Rugwiza's remnant family. This is the sad day when the wife of pastor Rugwiza and his first-born child, together with church choir members, were killed. They were on their way to mark the end of the mourning period. The church, family, and friends ended the father and child's mourning period. This is a time when everyone comes together to close the funeral ceremonies. That Sunday, church choir members rented an SUV. Together with Pastor's wife, her firstborn teenager, and a Hutu driver, they were killed on the way to the ceremony. This was an ambush by Rwanda's hit squad. Also, two people who followed on a motorcycle were killed. It was a very sad day.

In less than two months, an entire family was erased from the face of the earth, and in a country that is believed to be developed such as Rwanda (as they boast). But what kind of development can a country have where the government kill their own citizens? Within two months, innocent people were denied the right to live. This story was never written in the media! This story is one of thousands of what many people in Rwanda have gone through and are still experiencing.

Glory to God! Even in the midst of such cruelty, God always leave a witness as the French saying goes, "les murs ont les oreilles" meaning "even walls have ears." So, even walls can listen. One of pastor Rugwiza's children survived and made it overseas so one day she will be able to tell the story. Watching the tragedies, she did not understand what everything meant. She had been asking, "Hey, when they put my dad in that box, I never saw him again. Now they have put mom and my siblings in the box also, do you think that they will come any time soon?"

Tears rolling down, a brother responded, "My beloved child, what is happening here is beyond words. Let's pray!" How do you answer a question like this? How do you comfort a child who loses their entire family so cruelly?

26 years after the Genocide, with a fully-functioning government, you can see that the killings are still going on. In fact, they never stopped but took a different form. Can someone truly stop the genocide and fail to stop sporadic killings within the country he won? Or could it be that he who also killed during the genocide just continued to do it in the aftermath?

There are killings outside Kigali, in many remote areas, where they do their dirty work. But every killing must be well planned, done as top secret, and all evidence must be destroyed.

"Pastor Christine, I cannot tell you much from this side of the world. It is another world. All I can tell you is, they have made us dumb. They have cut out our tongues. We cannot tell you what is going on," said one of my old colleagues.

Rwandans have stories to tell! There are many Rwandans who know the cruelty of this regime firsthand. The day that Rwandans receive their freedom, they will tell the stories in so many books that we might not be able to count them.

I appeal to the international community, please conduct unbiased independent investigations into these killings. Have access to Rwanda. Talk to citizens without the presence of their oppressors. You will find out the world will not have enough staff to write those books nor enough papers to print them. It is beyond compare. If we fail to help, we have failed humanity as a whole and have lost our reason for living.

Vehicle that pastor Rugwiza's wife was in when the staged accident occurred.

THE CASE OF REVEREND BONIFACE KIMENYI.

In September and October, 2019, God allowed Iradukunda to be taken to different churches and allowed her to experience and survive atrocities so that these things could be reported to the world.

After surviving the killings at pastor Rugwiza's church and family, Iradukunda though still recovering had to flee to save her life. Her spiritual father and family were all dismantled within a short time and she had to start all over. In times like this, where does one go, and how does one manage to move forward?

For a season, she witnessed another massacre nearby where she was staying. This time, the government death squad targeted members of the Association of Pentecostal Churches in Rwanda (ADEPR), Gasave, in the village of Mukenke. An organized accident was staged against an ADEPR bus on their way to a concert. The bus was carrying members of Abarinzi choir and the choir president. They were ambushed and hit by the death squad. 22 choir members and the president of the choir were all killed on the spot. It is reported that they were mainly Hutus.

God's merciful hand protected Iradukunda and landed her in another church. This time, she was with Reverend Boniface Kimenyi who had a church in a Kigali suburb. Reverend Kimenyi was a bold man on the inside. He had opposed the government's gross injustice against all truth lovers. He had seen many pastors and believers alike being killed in unusual accidents and other ways. He openly began to express his concerns that the government was committing democide against any human right defender. He was determined to speak up more and to actually do something about it when all of sudden, on his way to run errands, they ambushed his car and smashed it, killing everyone aboard except Iradukunda.

She survived unscratched and protected by the mighty hand of God. She recalls seeing an angel who literally snatched her from that terrible accident and dropped her to a safe place. For weeks, Iradukunda did not keep in touch. She was speechless and shocked by what she had experienced.

I asked myself how in the world do these evildoers know precisely when people are traveling? Iradukunda revealed that censorship in Rwanda is real. The MTN phone company, instead of serving Rwandan customers, is being strictly monitored by the government, and is used as a tool to spy on citizens and to track them. They track the movements of people using their phone number.

In that accident, during the month of October 2019, Reverend Kimenyi did not survive. He died on the spot. The world lost such a great man.

Killings of Many Other Christians and the People of Good Faith

On February 13, 2020, 28 Christians were murdered. Among them was Edward Ngendahayo, a Hutu Christian who was married to former senator and ex-governor of Rose, a southern province. He was murdered by the regime in Kamonyi – Gitarama, in a fake accident. Early that day, the police only reported 7 dead, but 28 died in total. This was part of the ongoing campaign to murder Hutus and Christians.

On September 10, 2014, evangelist and prophetess Jane Uwimana was a powerful woman of God. One day she was invited to go preach in different places in Rwanda, and among them a military camp. It was said that during that time, she prophesied against the evil deeds by the regime. After preaching, she did not make it home. The next day, the police called one of her family members to go look for her corpse saying that a truck had hit her while she was riding a motorcycle. They showed them the corpse, but they did not see the motorcycle nor the truck. They simply told the family to pick up their dead.

A few years before Uwimana's death, there was a young man nicknamed Zacchaeus because he was short. He was from Cyangugu, Rwanda. He used to go in the streets of Kigali, prophesying and calling out the government telling them to repent. He was later jailed in a military camp and he finally disappeared. To this day, no one knows his whereabouts.

There are thousands upon thousands of cases of Christians who die this way inside Rwanda. The killings all happen in the remote areas, far from the sight of the public. "It is a daily occurrence," says everyone I have spoken to. They have told me similar stories of losing either spouses or children through the hands of state agents' death squads.

CHRISTIANS & HUTUS MASSACRES IN GASABO / RWAMAGANA

On January 3, 2020, at dusk, a massacre took place in Rwanda and it claimed the lives of many innocent people. This massacre was well planned and everything about it a top secret: no foreigner or local journalist were allowed in the area. Every phone they could get was confiscated, and no one was allowed to record, report, or say anything about this massacre. There was no media presence. Fear and intimidation were used on anyone who dared to stand up to this massacre. However, even the sky is watching. By God's providence, it was reported by an underground journalist. We owe it to those killed and their families, to say what happened!

This massacre occurred in the City of Kabuga, district of Gasabo and Rwamagana. This area is low rent, very populated compounds. The residents in this area are poor, mostly Hutus, persecuted Christians, and everyone who is considered as a second-class citizens of Rwanda. Yes, second class citizens exist in Rwanda – these are the ones with no rights! Some of you might have seen videos on social media of Rwandans whose homes were destroyed in December 2019. Those are second class citizens. They had their homes but the government came and destroyed them without compensation, without any mutual agreement . These second-class citizens have no rights to speech, they have no healthcare, no job, and they constantly live in fear because they are being hunted down constantly.

It all started on January 3rd 2020. Kagame's Rwanda State Agents came when it was getting dark and surrounded this area. All of sudden, without warning, explosives were thrown into homes where people were making their meals and preparing for the evening. A survivor from this massacre who chose to remain anonymous recounted the horror, "It was not just grenades, but it felt like some sort of a bomb."

As people began to flee the scene here and there, they were told by the state agents that it was the rebels who had attacked their residence. But something did not add up as these state agents began to confiscate phones so that no one was able to take pictures nor call the media or friends. People could not call relatives to say what took place. The state agents threatened that anyone who said a word of what took place, or report in in some way, would be killed. They also said that anyone who took a picture or video would be shot dead!

Journalists were not allowed to the area. Anyone outside the compounds were not allowed to get close. At first, it was counted that 21 people died on the spot, and there were many people in critical condition. Cars were destroyed and people lost their belongings. The casualties increased by the hour, and within 24 hours, there were already over 70 people dead!

"I survived these massacres in a miraculous way!" said another witness who lived in the compound and was able to reach out to our organization. "I had gone to do some errands and was supposed to come earlier but by God's providence, I stayed longer and visited some friends. When I came at dusk, the massacres were just happening!" Some of those in critical condition were taken away to never be seen again. Another witness shared how 'Agafuni', a gardening hoe usually used by RPF death squads, was being used to finish the weak and those in critical condition who did not die on the spot. They also threatened that anyone who would share what took place would be killed. They do not want anyone to share the truth. They also took away many people who survived these massacres and to this day nobody knows what has happened to them.

Why This Massacre

Besides the persecution of Christians who do not bend to Kagame's wishes, witnesses said they overheard the agents complaining that it was a Hutu quarter. This is an area where in the past Hutus lived. During the 94 war, the RPF took this area but after a legal battle after the genocide, they lost and it was restored to Hutus who were the original owners.

One witness said, "did you not see how they destroyed homes in December in the capital city of Kigali? It is the same thing they are doing here! These Kagame people have no love for the poor, nor for the Hutus! They blame them for every ill that happened to the country. The poor, the truth lovers, and the Hutus have no rights in Kagame's Rwanda."

Many Christians Were Killed, Including a Christian Journalist

This is an area next to the famous cave in Samatare of Rwamagana where Christians started flocking, especially after the closing of churches in Rwanda in 2018.

The next day of the massacre, a witness testified of seeing a body by the sidewalk. When they looked closely, it was that of a Christian journalist Consolata Uwimana (Consolee). Uwimana worked as a Christian journalist and was from time to time on a Christian radio. She gathered the courage and decided to go nearby the area to report on this. These Kagame boys killed her and the next day, some Christians came and took her body away to bury her in honor. It was reported that Uwimana was a truthful journalist who was not afraid to speak the truth.

By Sunday, January 5th, those whose families had means had already began to bury their dead. Among them was Zakayo, who was a singer and also a deacon in a local church. There is also another Tutsi pastor who was killed, and his crime was that he was giving preparatory teaching to 47 disciples, getting them ready for baptism, and he was told that he should not pray nor baptize Hutus.

An underground journalist witnessed a young man in his early twenties by the roadside, who said, "Dear God, we have zero voice in this country, there is no one to speak up for us. I did not choose to be born in Rwanda, dear God. I did not get to choose my race. God please help me. I have been wandering from place to place in my own country! Being hunted down day and night like a criminal before I even became a teenager. I was born after the genocide! Dear God, please, we have been oppressed beyond understanding! We did not choose to be born in Rwanda. Dear God, please hear us and help us!"

When the Pictures Came Out

For many years, thousands upon thousands inside Rwanda

and DRC were brutally murdered. It was very hard to share those experiences with the outside world, and oftentimes, people would not believe. In recent years, however, thank God for Rwanda's high speed internet. Pictures began to surface via WhatsApp and social media. Rwandans began to use their phones to capture moments of torture and abuse by the state agents, to show the world what they were going through.

When the pictures of their abuse surfaced on internet, Kagame's online army were mad. Very angry, they let out insults. They rushed as a swarm of bees and they began commenting with blatant lies and innuendos, attacking whoever posted pictures of their killings or abuse. They would also justify the killings. If there is anything these murders do not want to see, it is their evil secrets being exposed.

On social media, by looking at the comments of the people you could see two groups: those who showed compassion towards the victim, and those who did not. For example, in the case of Mihigo we presented previously, instead of showing compassion or sympathy towards Mihigo, they showed joy, they justified why he was killed, saying, "He was friends with Rwanda enemies." As if to say 'yes, he died, but we warned him. He should not talk to those who oppose our president.' They would show no mercy whatsoever for the person they have eliminated. It reminded me the times of Solomon.

A story is told in 1 Kings 3, where two women came before King Solomon fighting over one living baby boy, each mother claiming "he is mine." The Bible says that they had given birth a few days apart and lived in the same house. One night, one of the women slept on the baby, killing him. The woman then came and stole the living baby while the mother was sleeping. In the morning, they argued over the baby each saying, "the living one is my son," while the other also said, "no he is mine."

When they came before King Solomon, each still claiming the living son as hers, Solomon said, "Get me a sword." So, they brought a sword before the king who said, "Divide the living child in two, and give half to the one and half to the other." One of the women said, "Oh, my lord, give her the living child, and by no means kill him." The other woman said, "Yes, he shall be neither mine nor yours, divide him!" Then the king knew the mother who showed compassion was the real mother. The murderers will show no compassion when the victims are being killed . The murderers have lost their human heart.

A video was posted of a District Administration Security Support Organ (DASSO) beating a helpless woman to death. DASSO are local defense forces that support the police and they are oftentimes involved in extrajudicial executions. When such a video would be posted on internet, Kagame's online army would not show a single compassion.

When we saw the pictures of two innocent children being thrown in the river while their father was killed, instead of showing the heart of compassion, instead of speaking up for the victim, instead of speaking up for the person being tortured, instead of shedding tears to see another human enduring torment like that of hell, the Kagame goons came fighting, protecting the country, and justifying the murders. "This is not real," they insisted.

For the first week, they were upset that the truth was being exposed. Then, after a while, because more pictures kept coming, God exposing more of their evil deeds, they came up with deeper deceptions, to photoshop each one of them and insert them in the old magazines of their own.

There are many videos and photos out there on the internet that show those atrocities. There are also many videos and pictures buried in the heart of Rwanda. But there are also pictures underground inside Rwanda. Rwandans are seated on some of most heartbreaking stories and testimonies on earth. For the moment, they stay quiet because they are afraid. The day when God makes a way for them to share, the whole world will be shocked.

In His Speeches, Kagame Brags He is Not Afraid to Kill

It is September 11, 2016. Inside the packed auditorium of the Kigali Convention Center, Rwanda President Paul Kagame is addressing an estimated 2,000 young people who had completed training in the ruling party's ideological school, Itorero, and he is bragging of how he is not afraid to kill[2].

"So, do you think that you can come and destroy this building? No, I must kill you before you do so," he said.

The youth are all clapping their hands enthusiastically in unison as if drunk from being in the presence of a tyrant. I wonder if they really heard what he just told them. The president continues standing on a podium and behind him a backdrop reads, #MeetThePresident"

Kagame continued, *"There are those who are ashamed to make such a bold statement but I am not. I will get on you, even our critics, who are freely speaking from abroad, talking about nonsense, maybe they do have the right to do so, but there is a red line drawn, to not cross. As long as you have not crossed this line, I leave you alone... but when you cross that line, you will not know what has brought you down, what has hit you..."*

This is not the first time the president is encouraging the people to practice extrajudicial killings. On June 5, 2014, while addressing residents of Nyabihu District, Northern Rwanda, President Kagame said, in response to criticisms by the U.S. government about enforced disappearances by security agents, *"We will continue to arrest suspects and, when needed, shoot in broad daylight those threatening to destabilize the country."*[3]

In another speech, at a National Prayer Breakfast, a place where many pastors and ministers of God have gathered together, Kagame said, *"Anyone who betrays our cause or wishes our people ill will fall victim. What remains to be seen is how you fall victim."*[4]

Lord, Save Us from a President Who Kills

Please, pray with us: Oh, dear heavenly Father, please have mercy on Rwanda. This is a place you have prepared for all Rwandans to live and enjoy but Lord, many have been deprived of their motherland. Oh, dear Lord, what sin have Rwandans committed that they would be allowed to have a president who does not love his own people? What have they done to inherit a president who kills his own subjects? Oh, dear Lord, hear our prayers, we beseech you, and save Rwandans from a president and a government that kill their own citizens!

3

INSIDE TORTURE CHAMBERS

———

THE CASE OF BARAFINDA SEKIKUBO FRED

The following testimony comes from interviews Barafinda held with the press, his social media accounts and also from talking to him directly. Links to those interviews are provided in the footnotes.[1]

Barafinda's Testimony

Barafinda Fred Sekikubo is a Rwanda politician. He is also a Christian with a rock-like faith. He is known by many Rwandans as "The Good Politician." He has a big dream to become the president of Rwanda. In 2017, Barafinda began a political campaign to run against President Paul Kagame but was barred by the government's right wing, National Electoral Commission, on technical grounds. The commission also barred candidacies of other true challengers against Kagame like Diane Rwigara. Barafinda did not get discouraged by this. He decided to move forward as a peaceful activist inside Rwanda, to fight injustice and the rights of all Rwandans. From then on, a journey of the cross began for him. He was arrested and imprisoned several times. He was tortured and nearly killed. Following is his testimony.

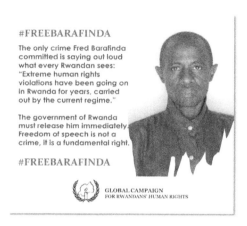

#FREEBARAFINDA

The only crime Fred Barafinda committed is saying out loud what every Rwandan sees: "Extreme human rights violations have been going on in Rwanda for years, carried out by the current regime."

The government of Rwanda must release him immediately. Freedom of speech is not a crime, it is a fundamental right.

#FREEBARAFINDA

GLOBAL CAMPAIGN
FOR RWANDANS' HUMAN RIGHTS

Barafinda Fred Sekikubo is the president of the RUDA party. In 2017, he began a political campaign against President Kagame but was barred by the government right wing National Electoral Commission. After multiple tortures, Rwanda government has forced him into a mental health facility against his will.
#FreeBarafinda
Barafinda Facebook Picture / Global Campaign for Rwandans' Human Rights

Terrorism at Home in Rwanda

"I was kidnapped several times! Five times, I was taken to their prisons, in a place where they torture people. But God allowed it, that I would be moved around and taken to different torture sites so that I may later tell the world. I was abused beyond comprehension in all sorts of various tortures. No ordinary torture. I would say, debasement, dehumanization," Barafinda testified . "You look at the people who inflict those tortures and you wonder if they are truly human beings!"

Barafinda asked his tormentors, "When you do such wicked crimes and the people die, do you bother informing their families? Or, do you take the body back to their families? Tell me, what happens?"

"Listen to this one," they mocked. "We will throw you in a trench and bury you there! Are you worthy of anything? No, nothing, you are worthless," they said. "I listened, I observed, and I found out these people are just terrorists!"

"The way I was persecuted, abused, being dehumanized, being shown no love, no mercy whatsoever, for a human being created in God's image is beyond compare. Here, people are being abused just because of the way they look, or because of their size, height, and weight. Based on the way God created a person, which none of us get to choose," he said. "When I looked at my tormentors, I looked at them as human beings, but I could not find a human heart in them. Listen to me. I have seen many things and I have been taken to the most powerful, wicked prisons in this country. Now, I call them factories where all manners of wickedness are invented!"

Barafinda added, "I have seen those who abuse you without

thinking that you are a human being! I have seen those who are consumed with love of self and they hate everybody else. I was abducted, my family did not know where I was. They did not know my whereabouts."

Abusing Barafinda's Family

"They blocked the way to our house. My wife (whom he calls first lady) and our children were always surrounded by difficulties. They caused us sorrow. They isolated us. They fought us, they sought to bring us down. This is their landmark. They make everybody hate you. Your tormentors appoint themselves as your spokesperson. While we did not send them to speak on our behalf, they went, speaking ill on our behalf. We have encountered sorrow upon sorrow within our motherland!"

Barafinda's Torture at "Chez Gacinya"

Gacinya means the hitman. "Chez Gacinya" is one of the unofficial most notorious detention centers in Rwanda, where severe tortures take place. It is named after General Gacinya Rugumya whom president Kagame named to be the head of the Criminal Investigation Division (CID) of the police, and then at one time named military attaché at the Rwandan embassy in Washington, D.C. He is known all over Rwanda for his merciless torture, incarcerations, and killings.

"While incarcerated at Chez Gacinya, I met one of the police officers who is also my neighbor in Rwanda, in Kanombe of Nyarugunga," Barafinda recounted. "There also came another police officer who had clear skin, that people called him Mzungu (i.e. the Whiteman). He came there, decked with many stars on his shoulders. He was a high-ranking officer, insolent and full of pride. He looked and looked at me, examining me like you would a worthless dog."

"Both of them, after examining me, left the place. I was taken upstairs to the office of Enoch Mugume, who had put my information into the system the last time I was imprisoned there. He is the one who interviewed me, and asked me many questions from the time I was born to now. He asked what kind of person I was. He had torturing tools to tell you how he will beat you and break you without mercy."

"Sure enough, he had no mercy," Barafinda said. "He tortures you, and you wander what kind of person he is since his existence? You just wonder! In that office, he works with Antoine Gasasira. Antoine had interviewed me before in a safe house in Kicukiro center, a place where they hold political prisoners. In the backyard of where I was imprisoned, there is a special prison level three, where you cannot sit down or stand. It is a place which is very cold, infested with mosquitoes. It has long walls. All these things, I have seen and I was tortured through them. So, when I was taken at Chez Gacinya, they took me to the hospital where they gave me drugs against my will. They put me on IV's. After that, instead of taking me home, they took me again to Chez Gacinya. I remember these things very well. These are terrorist activities, and they do it and get paid from citizen's taxes, Imagine getting paid to kill citizens!"

Illegally Detained for 120 Days in Undisclosed Location

"After these two police officers at Chez Gacinya left, Enoch and Antoine took all my phones and my IDs. They labeled them with my name, they called Desire who used to guard me day and night. Desire came, called in his colleague by name of Mugume, he entered the room and removed his civilian clothes and put on a police uniform. Mugume took off my red tie, Desire took one of my hand and held me, and Mugume took the other hand and they took me out. My eyes were blinded with the red tie. They took me downstairs and into a vehicle and called their buddies telling them, "Prepare those tools, the nice stuff. Prepare them well, we are coming." So, they were asking them to prepare a special prison for me where they would put me. They started the car, and in handcuffs, they took me away."

"They took me where I did not know, but I could guess. I know the roads here very well. In my brain, I would imagine where they were taking me. After they got to a rough dusty road, by Sonatube, nearby Chez Lando, they went as if they were going to Remera stadium. They reached a certain place and it was at night. We entered this place; they parked the car and took me out and carried me again upstairs of a certain building. I kept counting how many stairs. The door opened, they removed the tie they had blinded me with, and they had already taken off my shoes. They lit a lamp and threw me in a cell and closed the metallic door. I was illegally detained there for 120 days without anyone knowing my whereabouts!"

When Barafinda's family looked for him and went to inquire at the police station, they were told that they did not know his whereabouts. Barafinda said, "This is how our government works. They lie. They deceive."

Barafinda continued his story. "After like three months or so, one of the people told my wife, 'Go look for your husband, there is a certain building with many stories, with tinted windows.'"

"My dear friend, look what is going on here – my own neighbor police officer denied that they do not know where I was, but this place is very known by the police and a Samaritan friend gave the right tip to my wife. The police come back and forth to this place, so why did my neighbor not tell the truth my wife? Oh, dear listeners, what do you call this? Tell us, what is going on in this country? The people who are supposed to protect you are the ones betraying you!"

"There was a time later, when the law enforcement came to our home. They took our family's health insurance cards away. We had no idea why, or what they did with our cards. Later, they brought them back and gave the cards to my wife."

"Again, another time, I was kidnapped," Barafinda stated. "They took me to Kibagabaga. While there, they took my ID and began entering my information into their computer system. All of sudden, I saw that all our information downloaded into their programs automatically, but I never gave it to them before. So now you understand that when they took our health insurance card, they put our information into the system. They wrote down that they will give us drugs against our will, poison us to kill us all, on top of kidnapping me, harassing us, persecuting us!"

Barafinda testified that the system did everything they could to bring him down and to uproot him. He had built a very nice, big home in the area where he lives. He said he was among the first residents in this area, and his house was so big that people driving by would wonder if it was a church. Barafinda said he was denied water and electricity, though they paid to have those things installed. For twenty years, Barafinda has had no electricity nor water while everyone else in the neighborhood has it.

Even the city threatened to block them by using neighbors. They blocked the entryway, he said, adding, "We have been harassed and have gone through hell. We have received over 220 official summons and papers. We have gone to the institution in charge of justice, including the presidency of Rwanda. We have written to them, asking that we be acquitted and given justice but it was in vain. Instead, they harassed us the more. Those who were supposed to protect us became our tormentors, our kidnappers. These are the things that are happening here inside Rwanda. It is in this way, I founded the Rwanda Revolutionary United Democratic Advancers (RUDA), so that we can uproot this evil from our country."

Not Only Christians But Muslim and Other People of Faith Are Persecuted

"Another time, I was taken to Emmanuel Gasana, Inspector General of Rwanda National Police. Right there was a big Muslim guy. He looked like a wealthy person. I witnessed his abuse. They had kidnapped him and handcuffed him. I do not know where they got him from, but by the time they got him to the police station, he was already badly beaten and tortured. He looked weary. Someone came and handed him a letter to read. While reading it, tears began to roll down his cheeks, and after reading it he fainted! It was a letter that sentenced him to death," Barafinda said with sadness.

"In a short time after reading the letter, many cars pulled in. They came rushing, turned here and there, and they parked.

Those who were in those vehicles came, took him, and put him on the roof of the car while he was handcuffed. They just threw him on top of the car and they drove the car off at a higher speed. His body fell down and they shot him with many bullets. This is how he was killed! This is how he died! After this, they began to tell their lies. "Oh, you know, he was trying to escape from the prison. 'Oh, he was trying to break the rules and flee." It was all lies. He was wearing a Muslim hat. This Muslim who is also a child of God! Oh, the wickedness of this government. Can you believe the people who do this are paid by the government? This is injustice. This is what made me stand up and fight this injustice. The prophet Mohamed taught the Muslim to be humble and to endure when death comes. This brother was shot and he died in dignity!"

"There was a police officer who stepped forward and spoke up for him. He said that he knew that this Muslim was unjustly sentenced. I believe this police officer was used by God. It is a testimony of his innocence before God. No crime will go unpunished even if it takes time according to human standards. As the saying goes, 'Imana ihora ihoze,' God revenges, quietly and slowly, without having to hurry."

"Our dear government, you know not what human rights means! You know not the weight of life God gave to the human being, whom He loves. You do not know how precious life is. God created this Muslim man, he became an adult, he worked hard, went to school, and became such a dignified noble person, and you have killed him in this way, just like that! I am here to tell you that his blood will not go in vain, his blood is against you, and your children, and your great grandchildren, to the tenth generation. These are the curses you are piling upon yourself."

"This incident showed again the lack of justice among those who call themselves our leaders. This is not leadership. Someone was denied justice in broad day light. The poor Muslim man's family, his wife, and children, and friends, they will never see him again. Some people might think he is still alive, while he is no more. These things are happening in broad day light, right here in our city, and it shows that there are many people who have died this way."

"We must say no to such deeds; we say no to such wickedness. There is no wickedness beyond this. Do not kill democracy. Do not lie to the world that we are a democratic nation. Rwanda is below zero when it comes to democracy. There are no human rights in Rwanda. There is no one who cares about it. There is no justice whatsoever."

At Gacinya, Women Are Not Spared

Barafinda continued, "When I was at Chez Gacinya, behind the house where I was imprisoned, there is also a kitchen. I remember the person they shot to death there! The blood came, gushing, streaming down from the prison cell all the way to the outside. And they brought water and swept it away. When I was being interviewed, in the darkness of the night, I witnessed this. After killing that person, they brought in a woman and no one knows where she is to this day."

"Even the police officers are not spared. One day, they brought that handsome policeman whom I told you had clear skin. They brought him and put him in jail there! He was a handsome man, tall. They jailed him there. Later on, I saw him at Kanombe and they had cut one of his legs off! Before, he was a healthy young-looking man and he had two legs, standing on his own."

"Now, he is in Kanombe where I saw him and has only one leg! All these wicked deeds, all these prisons throughout the country where thousands of innocent people are, I Barafinda Sekikubo Fred, when I become the president of Rwanda, I will come and close them. I will deliver Rwanda's people. I will close these prisons and safe houses. I Barafinda, the good international politician, I will stand up and defend human rights everywhere. I will rise up and defend the rights of everyone, including you my tormentors. We will outdo your wicked deeds by our righteous deeds and lovingkindness." (Note: Barafinda gave permission to retell his story, with some editing for space considerations.)

This is the reality of what is going on in Rwanda. This is the real Rwanda, a place where people have been denied their basic human rights. In order to mislead people, Rwanda spends so much money advertising on internet and social media – projecting herself to be a paradise on earth. "Come visit Rwanda." "We are the first country in Africa to do this…We are the cleanest city in Africa…" The regime focuses on showing off the new thing going on here and there, but they do not care about their human rights abuse.

Deceiving Through Advertorials

My friend David Himbara   said, "General Paul Kagame has found a new way of spreading propaganda that he turned Rwanda into an economic lion. He is placing advertorials in U.S. media. What is an advertorial? The term "advertorial" combines the words "advertisement" and "editorial." An advertorial reads like a publication's own content but is, in fact, a paid advertisement."[2]

Besides advertising, much money is spent on lobbyists, among them public relations firms. There are also senators who are great supporters and promoters of Kagame. They have praised him for his fake economic miracles, and thus have emboldened him to move forward and kill democracy in Africa though it might not be their intention.

Beloved senators, and also Tony Blair and Bill Clinton,

think of all the people being killed in Rwanda everyday by this one man's rule. Think about the prisons that are full of innocent people. Think of the multitudes of Christians who have been martyred, persecuted, and killed. Think about the human rights of Rwandans which have been trampled on by Kagame. Read the stories of the people here and consider your actions. Together we can end this modern-day slavery happening inside Rwanda and bring forth everlasting peace and democracy.

Barafinda Testimony: Buried Alive and Surviving

Barafinda also testified how he was forcibly taken to a mental health hospital against his will just because he dared to say, "Thus says the Lord to President Kagame…" Once in the mental hospital he found many other young people who have been forced there; the only crimes these young men had committed was to prophesy to the president of Rwanda saying, "God sent me to you and here is the message." The mental health institution claims to give them an injection, "So that they no longer hear the voice of God!"

"I was imprisoned. Handcuffed hands and feet. I was laid in a coffin while still alive! But did they kill me? No, because God protected me! Yes, they put me in a coffin," Barafinda says. "For two weeks, they left me there but when they came back, I was still alive! Alive because God protected me!"

Barafinda talks about how God allowed for him to be imprisoned and to be taken from different torture sites. They could not bear his presence in prison, so they began to take him from Chez Gacinya to other safe houses, from place to place. They did not know what they were doing. They did not know that God was in this. God was giving him a tour of their torturing sites so that he can tell the world, but they had no clue. These things have been going on for many years since the Rwandan Patriotic Front (RPF) took power.

"The Rwanda Investigation Bureau and Directorate of Military Intelligence is but a Rwanda Killing tools," he said. "They have tortured so many people and now they are ashamed. That's why they drive cars with darkly tinted windows. They fear to see those whom they have wronged, they also fear their families and friends."

Another Incident – Spared from Death

Barafinda said, "After my candidature to the presidency, they put me through many trials. When I was at Chez Gacinya torture center, three soldiers almost killed me. Three of them came, and the one leading the way was the angriest of them all. Amid their anger, one in the middle rose up and killed the one leading the way. He fell at the door and the blood gushed out of him, dripping into the coffin where they had laid me! The one in the back then turned and shot dead the one who was in the middle. Two people died right there on the spot, killing each other. Those two who died became my scapegoats. This happened right at Chez Gacinya."

"When They Torture You, They Tell You to Not Say A Word"

"Time came for me to be released. Before I left that place, I told them I have called this place the University of Understanding," he recalled. "They did not understand what I meant. They thought I was consenting to my crimes and giving them compliments. However, I was talking to them like a wise elder man — that what I have seen, what I have experienced is like a university to me! My eyes opened, and I gained understanding. I have experienced severe torture firsthand and when I become president, I will tell the leaders do's and don'ts. I will banish torture forever!"

"Thank you for allowing me to tell my testimony," Barafinda concluded. "I have only shared a little bit. May Jesus Christ come and deliver all these victims, whether Christians or not. All those who are longing for deliverance, may God come and deliver them. May God come and bless us all!"

4

CHURCH IN THE WEST UNKNOWINGLY FUNDING ANTI-CHRIST AGENDA

Origin: Kagame's Grudges Against Christianity

When the first missionaries arrived in Rwanda around 1900, Kagame's ancestors, who were the ruling class, rejected Christianity. In November 1931, King Musinga, an ancestor of Kagame, was deposed by the Belgian administration. He was replaced by his son, Charles Mutara Rudahigwa, who had secretly become a Christian. He was the first Rwandan king to become a Christian and to be baptized. During his reign, in 1946, he dedicated Rwanda to Christ, effectively making Christianity a state religion.[1]

Publicly, Kagame does not show to the West that he is anti-Christian. He knows well that all the aid to help Rwanda comes from the western countries, which are usually Christian nations. Outside, he seems nice to Christians but his actions and public speeches towards Christians show otherwise. Kagame has always held grudges against the Catholic church. In his speech, and even in his newspapers, he has constantly criticized the church for nurturing genocide planners and, in 1994, for helping the government implement the genocide, but The Bible, in Daniel 8:23-24, warns us of "a fierce king, a master of intrigue who will rise to power. He will become very strong, but not by his own power. He will cause a shocking amount of destruction and succeed in everything he does. He will destroy powerful leaders and devastate the holy people. He will be a master of deception and will become arrogant; he will destroy many without warning. He will even take on the Prince of princes in battle, but he will be broken, though not by human power."

Part of this prophecy was fulfilled during the reign of Antiochus IV Epiphanes, the Hellenistic king who destroyed many Jews. History repeats itself, and Hitler walked in the way of Epiphanes. Now, Kagame has picked up the baton, and if what citizens inside Rwanda are saying is true, then it makes Hitler a novice compared to Kagame.

There is a silent yet real persecution of Christians going on inside Rwanda. This persecution is worse because the outside world is mostly clueless. Thousands upon thousands have died without anyone responding to their SOS. The year 2018 saw a great persecution of Christians in Rwanda, but 2019 was the worst year of persecution I have ever heard of. Those who survived the killings and the massacres were told to never say a word, and if they dare, they are dead!

RWANDA

Disappearing Christians

Rwandan police catch Christians praying inside a cave. In early 2018, Rwanda outlawed meeting, praying or worshipping outside of government-approved buildings.

Since 1994, more than 123 religious leaders have been killed in Rwanda.

President Paul Kagame closed more than 6,000 churches in the first half of 2018, while banishing *Human Rights Watch* and "unfriendly" foreign journalists, and targeting free speech. Those who dare challenge him "disappear" – either exiled, imprisoned or simply murdered.

SAVE US

Save The Persecuted Christians

"The People of the Cross"
https://savethepersecutedchristians.org/the-people-of-the-cross

Cracking Down on Churches

In early 2018, Rwanda banished Human Rights Watch from the country and outlawed public meetings, praying, or worshiping outside of government approved buildings. Then, Rwanda began to close thousands of churches over a short period. During the Rwanda National Leadership Retreat on March 1, 2018, talking about churches that were closed in Kigali alone, President Kagame said, "*Seven hundred churches in Kigali? Are these boreholes that give people water? I don't think we have as many boreholes. Do we even have as many factories? But 700 churches, which you even had to close? This has been a mess!*"

Within three months, more than 8,000 churches were closed citing building and safety code violations. But at the same time, the government cracked down on groups caught worshipping outside. For example, in the Northern Province that is mountainous, with a history of people praying outdoors, Kagame declared this practice illegal.

Some churches were closed even when they met all the requirements. Such was the case of an American-owned Amazing Christian radio and church. The radio had its license revoked. Missionary Greg Schoof, the director of Amazing Grace Christin Radio said that both Rwanda Media Council (RMC) and Rwanda Utility Regulation Authority (RURA) did not respect Rwanda laws in closing his radio and church. Later on, missionary Schoof was expelled by the Rwanda government.

Slowly, Christian programs on the radio and TV began to be replaced by traditional religion that is linked to worshipping of spirits and witchcraft. World Watch Monitor called it an effort by the government to make it an aggressive secular stance. A nation that knew revival once, a nation that was over 80 percent Christian was made secular overnight! World Watch Monitor also noted that there had been a marked increase in secularism in the government.

As of 2018, the regime began to introduce laws that are hostile towards Christianity. They outlawed preaching unless you have degree in theology. They also outlawed long fasting, prayers in many government buildings, and began taxing tithes and offerings. Words referring to Christian faith were removed from the Constitution and the government began to control everything in the churches.

Imprisonment and Kidnapping of Pastors

In the midst of cracking down on churches in 2018, Rwanda officials arrested six pastors for assembling without permission: Bishop Innocent Rugagi, Pastor Charles Rwandamura, Pastor Fred Nyamurangwa, Reverend Emmanuel Ntambara, Pastor James Dura, and Pastor Emmanuel Kalisa Shyaka. They were all accused of plotting to defy government orders. Although the pastors have since been released, a senior church leader explained that the arrest served as a stern warning to others to not resist the move of closing churches. From then on, many Christians began to contact us via social media sending their SOS, saying how their loved ones were disappearing or being killed in accidents and other unimaginable ways at the hand of government agents.

A Word to the Churches

Beloved friend, especially Christians in the West, I have shown you the evil deeds of this regime with tangible proof. I have clearly shown you the persecution being done against your very own brothers and sisters in Rwanda, and I am about to reveal more. As you read, you can see the working of anti-Christ spirits in this beautiful nation. But will it shock you even more if I tell you who is the co-sponsor of these evil deeds?

There was a woman who wrote a book about Rwanda's genocide and she became famous as a result. This woman is a personal friend to President Kagame and his wife, and works for them promoting Kagame and Rwanda. Following the writing of her book, she was a most sought-after speaker by many people in the West but especially churches.

Everywhere she went to speak, she would introduce the church to the government of Rwanda and therefore thousands of churches began to link to Rwanda thinking they are helping a great government. But I have shown you the truth and what this regime is really doing.

The Church Is Sponsoring anti-Christ Government

Imagine Satan doing his evil deeds, anti-Christ persecuting our brothers and sisters; and you being the co-sponsor of these deeds! I did not know all of these things, but God in His grace and in His mercy opened my eyes to see. In 2013, I had a face-to-face encounter with God where he clearly showed me these things. Not only that, but he has shown me thousands of Rwanda martyrs and countless numbers of people, a sea of people, who have lost their lives through this reckless government.

Imagine Satan doing his dirty work and you being his sponsor, being used without having the knowledge that you are being used by the devil. Of course, no true Christian will do that knowing it is the enemy; but the enemy blinds and deceives by enticing and telling you they are doing great things while the money is channeled to slaughter God's people.

Remember that in the beginning Hitler himself used Christians to his own advantage. Remember when they said "One Nation! One God! One Reich! One Church!" In the end, God had mercy, Christians began to see but they had already joined Hitler in his evil work.

Professional Deceivers

So, my beloved friend, remember that all that shines is not gold. Checking and examining everything is very important in order to not be deceived. When you go to Rwanda, you might not see these things at first because there is a higher form of deception. You should beware of any churches recommended by the government. I was told of a certain Charles Mugisha's church, that it's the only church that Rwanda's foreign affairs ministry recommends diplomats and expatriates attend. This was done under the directive of Paul Kagame. So, check and examine before you pour your financial support out there.

Kagame wants to be international. Kagame wants to rule the world. And he works hard with lobbyists to get him everywhere. At the National Prayer Breakfast in Washington, D.C., Kagame's wife is often one of the speakers. A brother who wrote this, "The irony of all this, is the hypocrisy of Jeannette Kagame. She preached on reconciliation, love, and unity during National Prayer's Breakfast in Washington, D.C. in 2020. This is a woman who has initiated assassinations of innocent citizens, plundering of the economy, racketeering in DR Congo, installed hatred within society, and encouraged political intrigues, especially within the ruling party."

Who invited her to come and lead prayer and preach? It must be Christians because this is a prayer breakfast.

A Word of Warning to Christians from Missionary

Paul Philipps[2]

Paul Philipps warned Christians, saying, "As a former missionary in Rwanda, I can report that the problem of Kagame's persecution and control of his people has taken place throughout his rule. This man is often celebrated in the West and within Rwanda. But Rwandans know they have no freedom to speak without fear of disappearance at the hands of Kagame's goons. The government sends pastors away once a year to retraining camps to instruct them on obedience to the government – on pain of death is the subtext of the retraining."

"Sadly, many churches in the U.S. enter ministry in Rwanda not knowing the problems. Case in point, go to Saddlebackcanwetalk.us and read clear documentation that shows how Rick Warren has befriended Kagame, defended Kagame, and financially supported Kagame's war for minerals in Congo while ignoring the appeals of Congolese pastors."

Philipps ended by suggesting, "Anyone with a missionary friend of interest in Rwanda needs to read Timothy Longman's excellent book 'Christianity and Genocide in Rwanda', which documents the horrors of how poor missions work in Rwanda has set the stage for three Genocides."

5

EXPERIENCING RWANDA'S 1990 WAR & KILLINGS

———

RECALLING THE FOUR YEARS OF WAR AND GENOCIDE

From the years 1990 - 1994, while living in my beloved home country of Rwanda, my eyes witnessed the manifest presence of evil. At first what I saw seemed to be like a very long dream, but it was not. The reality was before my very eyes! War, extreme hatred, and fear surrounded all of us who lived in Rwanda. People were killing one another!

Yes, those who lived in Rwanda at the time saw the face of evil. We saw death taking the lives of many through individual and mass killings. We saw death prematurely taking the lives of our beloved, young and old alike. A great number of us lost parents, siblings, relatives, and friends. In fact, I can barely think of any family that did not lose anyone in Rwanda at that time. Some of those who were not killed in the 1994 Rwanda genocide were killed on the battlefields, as Rwanda had been at war since

1990. Many of those who escaped the Rwanda genocide and death from the battlefield were killed by Rwanda's Kagame politics of revenge and elimination inside and abroad, while others died from plagues in the aftermath of the Rwanda genocide.

I would have died, too, but somehow my life was preserved. During the war and the 1994 genocide, many times I asked God, "Why me, why me, Lord? What have I done or given to you so that my life is preserved?"

At the beginning of the genocide, my elder sister, Jeanne Françoise Nakure, and her entire family were taken captive and killed a few hours after I left their home. On another occasion, while caught up in the war, a building blew up a few minutes after I left it, destroying everything and everyone in it. Another time, while riding with a friend, our car was stopped at a blockade. The RPF army ordered my friend to follow them and I never saw him again. He was taken captive, separated from his dear wife and two children under the age of four, and he was killed by this army. My two beloved brothers, Regis and Pascal, whom I had visited months earlier were shot to death. Their crimes were that they were born Hutus and had a good education. Many relatives and friends were killed in this manner as well.

"Why me? What have I given to You, O, Eternal God that I would survive?" For many years, I did not have an answer to this question until one day in December of 2019, when I clearly heard the voice of God telling me thus,

"For this reason, you survived
To make known the truth to the whole world
What you have seen, heard and experienced
Make it known to the whole world"

Many know only of the genocide's three perilous months, but today time has come for the whole world to know about Rwanda's 30 years of apocalypse.

So far, one side of the story of the Rwanda genocide was officially narrated and accepted, but time has come to expose the killings that took place in Rwanda not only in 1994, but from 1990 to today. Even today, as this book is being written, people inside Rwanda are being killed, slaughtered like something that has no value. These things that have not been made known, God said, "Proclaim them from the rooftops." The lies that have been told will be exposed – Time to unearth the truth that has been hidden and buried for so long has come. Time to expose the deceit and lies have come.

May all freedom fighters and truth defenders stand as one and not watch a democide taking place like the former days of genocide. May all Christians and the people of faith stand up as one, pray and act for their brothers and sisters in Rwanda who are being persecuted. May Almighty God expose all the killings and abuse being done to the people of Rwanda and in the Great Lakes

Region and may He, together with us, lead truth and justice to victory!

Rwanda War and Genocide Summary

In Rwanda, since the beginning of time, there are three tribes: Hutu, Tutsi and Twa. The Rwanda war originated from the long-running conflict between the two main tribes, the Hutus and the Tutsi. At the time of the Rwanda war, the Hutus represented the majority of the population, estimated at about 85 percent. The Tutsis were next ranking at 14 percent and the Twa at one percent.[1]

The ancient Kingdom of Rwanda was ruled only by Tutsi kings. In1959, a Hutu revolution took place with the support of Belgium. It was said that Hutu activists, tired of being oppressed by Tutsis, began to burn Tutsi homes and fought against those who fought back, and ultimately established an independent, Hutu-dominated state in 1962. The revolution caused more than 100,000 Tutsi to flee to neighboring countries.[2]

Tutsis had an ambition to return to Rwanda. They formed armed groups, known as Inyenzi (cockroaches). They launched attacks into Rwanda with the largest invasion taking place in late 1963. These attacks were, however, unsuccessful. Some refugees, including Fred Rwigyema and Paul Kagame, fought in the Ugandan Bush War alongside with Yoweri Museveni. When he won the war in 1986, they became high ranking officers under his presidency. Later on, Rwigyema and Kagame used their military capability to turn the RPF into an army ready to attack Rwanda.[3]

The War Begins October 1, 1990

The Rwanda invasion began on October 1, 1990. It was led by General Major Fred Gisa Rwigyema, founder and leader of the RPF. This invasion started well for the RPF, but it suffered a blow when Fred Rwigyema was killed in action on the second day after the war had started. How Fred was killed remains a mystery but many people, after observing the pattern of killings in Rwanda, have no doubt who was the mastermind behind this.

At the time the war began, I was 18 years old and a student at Lycée Notre Dame d'Afrique – Nyundo Parish in Gisenyi prefecture. Normally, this was an all-girls school, but for the first time, in the third grade, a boy was allowed to be part of our school. The picture shows my classmates with one boy in an all-girls school of 600+. We were considered lucky being in the same classroom with this young man. In this classroom, there were 33 students. When I started at the Lycee, we were 45 students during the first year but every year, after the final exams, we lost students who could not make it to next level. We had to study hard to be approved to make it to the next level. By the time I reached the fifth grade, there were only 13 students left.

Class of 1990. 3rd Grade at Lycee Notre Dame d'Afrique – Nyundo

Today, as I think about it, I can see that as a result of this war I lost most of my schoolmates. I also lost many of my family members and friends through the Rwanda war, and then through the Rwanda genocide. Even now, I've lost many more through the Rwanda democide. Surviving this war does not make me a hero. This is not my story alone. This is a normal story to almost every Rwandan who survived these atrocities.

In the afternoon of October 2, 1990, as usual, I was in the classroom taking a history class when all of sudden it was announced that there has been a war on our Rwanda soil with an RPF invasion from the northeast part of the country. RPF attacked from Uganda and was fully supported by President Museveni.

When we heard this, it was bad news to almost everyone I knew. We lost heart. I had heard of wars, reported on wars, and I had learned of World War I and II, but never before had I thought I would live through a war!

During that year, I had begun to learn about the wars that tore Europe apart during World Wars I and II. I had read many books about these two wars and I knew this was not going to be a good thing for my beloved country, Rwanda. I was terrified!

The Rwanda We Knew
Organic, Beautiful and Peaceful

Rwanda was known as the country of a thousand hills. Beautiful, organic and pure. At age 18, I did not know what being on drugs was, I did not know what violence was. People lived in harmony. There was a proverb, "*Imana yirwa ahandi igataha i Rwanda*" meaning that God visits the earth throughout the day but His resting place is in Rwanda.

It was sung in one of the greatest hit songs at the time:

"*Oh, my beautiful dwelling place*

you are my paradise

That God chose for me"

Every food we ate was organic. It was almost impossible to find food that was not organic. We lived a simple life, without technology and TV, yet it was a beautiful happy life.

Prior to this war, Rwanda was a peaceful country. At age 18, I had not heard a single shot of a gun due to violence. I had not heard of people killing each other. The only time I witnessed a violent situation was when a gang member was caught in Kigali and people threw rocks at him. He ran away and by the time he came near our primary school of Rwankuba in the countryside, he was nearly dead. But strangers took him to the hospital, and he was taken care of.

Before the war, one traveled throughout the whole country unharmed, whether during the day or the night. We traveled without a single ID, no checkpoints except presidential palaces, or high-ranking officials offices and residences. There was no one saying you cannot leave the country. The sound of the gun and weapons were all foreign to us.

Unity

It was a united country until the war began. Families lived together. In the 80s, it was normal for people to have up to 10 or 12 children. Many children in a family were considered blessings. My parents had 10 of us, and what a blessing this was! What a joy, and what fun it was to live together and play together.

Many people lived under one roof where they shared things together, so this shaped us to be a people who yield to each other, who endures, who are not selfish, who share things together, and who wait. There was not much, but we were content. People lived a simple, beautiful life and we were taught the basics of the Bible and especially the Ten Commandments. In primary school, before the class began, we prayed. To the day I entered university at the age of 22, I had not seen anyone on drugs, I had not seen people depressed, I had not seen people divorcing. At that age, I probably knew only one family where the husband was divorced from the wife.

Ethnic

The three tribes: Hutu, Tutsi and Twa lived in Rwanda in harmony. The majority tribe of Hutu was 85 percent of the population at the time of war and genocide[4]. They occupied the most important positions in government and this sometimes caused people to be more aware of their tribes.

When it came to marriage, Hutus usually married Hutus, but it was common for Hutu men who were well of to marry Tutsis. Most times, Tutsi men married only within their tribe. By 1994, Rwanda's population stood at more than seven million people[4]. Prior to the colonial era, Tutsis generally occupied the higher levels in the social system and they were the ones in power . The line of the Kings issued only from the Tutsis. They were also herdsman, and the Hutus occupied the lower rank. They worked in the field and became servants to the Tutsis until the 1959 Hutu Revolution[5]. Within ethnic groups, there were also clans, which was a subdivision of the tribe one belonged to.

Growing up, each person knew whether they were Hutu, Tutsi, or Twa. You would learn that from your parents, but also when one reached the age to get an identification, the ID labeled you according to your tribe. This became a big problem when the war started.

At Rwankuba Primary School where I went for early learning, Hutu and Tutsi students sat side by side, played together, ate together, and we all lived in harmony. From time to time, in history, they would teach about the revolution of Hutus, and this could bring memories of the past for some people but where I went to school, this was not a big problem. The Tutsi population where I lived were very few, I would imagine less than two percent of the population.

In order to move from primary school to college, everyone would have to take the national exam and less than 10 percent made it into secondary school or college. Only the smart and powerful would make it to college.

Political and Socio-Economic

Up to the day I entered the university, I did not know any personal friends who had a television. One in 10,000 could afford to buy a car. You would not see people with electricity in their homes in the countryside. However, in the city people had electricity and running water. While living at Rushashi, we would walk a few kilometers to go fetch the water and the wood.

Each family had a parcel of a land and everyone cultivated their fields. In the fields people planted banana trees, plantain, coffee, vegetables and they raised cattle. Trees that bear fruit were planted everywhere. In our fields we grew lots of avocado trees, guava, oranges, mangoes, passion fruit, and all sorts of exotic fruit not seen in the West. There were vegetables of all kinds and people mainly cooked what they grew. People lived in harmony with one another, it was normal to not lock doors when you were not home, so people could come to your house and borrow salt, sugar even when absent they could serve themselves items people sold and leave money.

There was freedom of assembly. People met in houses of faith, in sports, in fellowship, for retreats, and in organizations of all types. While the freedom of speech might have been limited, all my life I had not heard of anyone imprisoned because of what they said. The country was still developing and had one national television by the time of the genocide. There was only one national radio station.

Most people had not traveled to the outside world, and most of us thought there was nothing wrong to have a leader for 20 years or so. We did not understand about democracy.

People trusted each other. We went to bed not worrying that someone would come and kidnap, kill, or steal. Prisons were empty. People who went to prisons were mostly gangs or very wicked people, but not for political reasons. I do not recall having acquaintances in jail, but everything changed on this one day – the day the war began and the dictatorship of Kagame stepped into the nation.

RPF Invasion, 1990-1994

After our history teacher announced that Rwanda had been invaded, for the next few days we began to hear news from the national radio that the people who had attacked were Tutsis from exile who formed a party called RPF. For some people like me, I did not know what this meant. I had vaguely heard that there were Rwandan Tutsis in exile. Before the death of my father, he told us of an uncle who lived in Uganda. He had lived there for many years and none of us had ever met him.

This war caused students to start thinking "Oh, what tribe am I?" People began to look at themselves and were conscious of who they were ethnically. This invasion brought division and, little by little, students began to hang out according to their ethnic groups.

The president of Rwanda at that time was Juvenal Habyarimana, a Hutu who had been the president since 1973. He was dearly loved by the majority of Rwandans. He was not a man of war, but of peace.

Rwandans were spoiled and so naïve! So naïve that we trusted everyone. Terrorism was foreign to every one of us. RPF took advantage of this innocence and they began to use children soldiers and people closest to you to kill, poison, and to commit atrocities. In one instance, at the Rwanda roadblocks (with the coming of the war, roadblocks were set up to make sure those who attacked were not disguised as civilians), a child soldier passed by the roadblock. In the real Rwanda, nobody could ever suspect a child. After the child passed the roadblock, he turned around and through grenades at those who were at the roadblock, killing people. RPF soldiers began to infiltrate everywhere. Because they dressed like civilians, it was important to check ID's.

At the beginning of the war, the government of Rwanda began to arrest some people whom they suspected to be accomplices with the invaders. They called them "ibyitso" meaning "traitors". Thousands of people were rounded up and were put in jail temporarily, and they were interrogated. Later on, however, they were released after interrogation. Among them, prominent Tutsi businessmen and women, and some Hutus as well. They were the ones whom they suspected were working with the Tutsis who had just attacked the country.

With RPF Invasion Came Killings

Killings were foreign on Rwanda soil. Everyone, regardless of their ethnicity, held life as something that is sacred. With the invasion of RPF however, on Rwanda soil for the first time, we began to hear about people being murdered, among them prominent politicians or citizens who had great accomplishments. People whom we held in high esteem, they began to eliminate them secretly. Prior to this invasion, I had traveled to almost all Rwanda Prefectures, and not once did I hear about killings or people being massacred. Rwanda was very safe.

It was so peaceful that even when Kagame was a youth, he used to come into Rwanda to visit Queen Rosalie Gicanda[6] in Butare. Queen Gicanda is said to be the aunt[7] of Paul Kagame, the sister of his mother Asteria. Unlike now, when Rwandans in exile cannot be safe if they dare put their feet inside Rwanda. Going inside Rwanda from abroad while one is not for Kagame is like going on a suicide mission. During the reign of Habyarimana, many Tutsis in exile used to come back and forth to visit their loved ones in Rwanda. They would go back into their country of exile without being harmed.

Young Kagame visiting Queen Rosalie Gicanda[8]

Killings Were the Tactics Used by Kagame

Rwanda is bordered by Uganda in the northern border, Tanzania on the east, Burundi on the south and the Democratic Republic of the Congo on the West. Uganda gave RPF free passage as they began a war against Rwanda. They came from the Northern province, which was known as Prefecture of Byumba.

Internally displaced persons fleeing RPF from Byumba began to scatter throughout Rwanda since October 1990. By 1993, the State Department estimated their number at 350,000 Rwandans, mostly Hutus, but also some Tutsis. They remained displaced as a result of the fighting between the Rwandan government and the RPF. We used to call them Refugees. These were very poor people who had become homeless and most of them lived in Nyacyonga Refugee camp. A country that had no clue of wars, of refugees; a country where everyone had his parceled land was filled now with displaced refugees and beggars, and they began to scatter throughout Rwanda. It was not common to see homeless people in Rwanda at the time. Rwandans began to grow weary of this situation that was created by the RPF. Many people in the back of their minds blamed the Tutsi who were helping the RPF. Rwanda citizens did not see any good coming from this war; all they saw were killings, death, rapes, children soldiers, and people who smoked and used drugs. These things were so strange and an abomination to Rwanda. Hutus, the majority of Rwandans inside the country, did not like the RPF culture, and they rallied together with President Habyarimana.

I had read and heard about the international laws regulating wars, namely the Geneva Convention, that in war it is forbidden to kill unarmed civilians. I had read that you do not kill someone who has surrendered with their hands held high. I had heard that you do not kill children, nor women, nor the aged, but this is not what Rwandans witnessed when Kagame's army moved in. The war was politically motivated and Kagame's troops killed whenever they saw that it could benefit them in any way. They killed unarmed civilians, they killed children, they killed people whose hands were held high in surrender. From 1990's to the end of genocide, that is what we witnessed.

Birth of Political Parties

Before the coming of the RPF invasion, it was a one man political party and one name on the ballot – Juvenal Habyarimana, and of course he won. Many Rwandans at the time had not traveled to the outside world and growing up without television made things worse, because people did not understand what democracy was. Most of the people did not see a problem with one name on the ballot.

With 85 percent of the population Hutus, Kagame knew if he goes the way of democracy he would not win. So, if he had a dream to become the president of Rwanda, he knew he would have to do things differently.

With the coming of the war, the door was open for opposition political parties. In November 1990, president Habyarimana allowed opposition political parties to organize. As a result, new parties were formed: the Democratic Republican Movement (MDR); the Democratic and Socialist Party (PSD); the Liberal Party (LP) and the Coalition for the Defense of the Republic (CDR). All these parties were opposed to the MRND except CDR. By 1993, some of the party leaders were ministers in the transition government to be formed.

Most people, regardless of their political party, began to recognize the atrocities of the RPF and they rose up and spoke against it. RPF responded by increasing their killings. In the beginning of May 1993, just before the signing of the Arusha Peace Accords, Emmanuel Gapyisi who was an active member of the MDR and former permanent secretary of the ministry of public works and infrastructure, called for a coalition movement against the RPF and MRND. Ten days after this speech, on May 18, 1993, Gapyisi was shot dead in front of his home in Kigali[9]. These killings were done by the RPF, though in his speech, Emmanuel was against both the RPF and MRND. RPF chose to get rid of someone just because of his opposing views. This would become Kagame's landmark. To this day, in Kagame's eyes, anyone with opposing views is considered as an enemy. According to the RPF oath (which is included in this book), any enemy must be crucified.

The Assassination of My Best Friend Jeanne D'Arc Mujawamariya

My best friend was a wise young lady. We met in our first year at the Lycee, in the same classroom. Jeanne d'Arc Mujawamariya was one of 43 students in the class. For almost every student, being many miles away from home for the first time, we became homesick. At times, being in this boarding school felt like being in a convent. Many of us had a culture shock. It was the first time to be away from our parents. It was the first time staying in a school where everything is taught in another language other than Kinyarwanda, our mother tongue. French was the language used at the Lycee to teach every subject except languages. For many of us, it was the first for almost everyone to have professors who were foreigners from Belgium and France.

For the whole semester, except for three or four times, we stayed inside this school with no physical contact with the outside world. One Sunday a month, the gate to the Lycee was open for our family and friends to come visit, but most of us had come from many miles away and few people were visited. In tough times, Mujawamariya brightened our days.

She began to distinguish herself as one of the top students. When it was very hard in classroom, especially the first semester, Mujawamariya was there not only for me, but for everyone in the classroom. She would gather us together and teach us wisdom, French, and English. By the time the war happened, Mujawamariya had become the dean's assistant for the entire school. She was from Byumba, the northern territory that was first occupied by the RPF. Her family became displaced because of the war.

When it was time to go to the fifth grade, Mujawamariya transferred to a new school in the southern part of Rwanda.

She continued to excel. The RPF had infiltrated the southern regions and they knew every leader student who was not a Tutsi. Mujawamariya did not have a group however, she always stood neutral and in truth. One weekend she was reported missing from school and after a while, her body was found floating in a nearby lake. News got to us that an RPF soldier who had infiltrated befriended her so that he could drown her in the lake. This method of drowning people is still being used in Rwanda. When we heard this bad news, we mourned her for many days. We knew that we would never see our best friend, Mujawamariya, again in the land of the living. I believe she made it to heaven, and I know that I will see her again.

Trying Peace Negotiation /Arusha Accords

Within two years of war, the president of Rwanda showed his willingness to sit down with RPF at the negotiation table. He chose to sit down with people who came killing. He went an extra mile to do this because he wanted peace and not a war. This was a lengthy process, involving the Rwanda government, the RPF, and the opposition leaders. This process led to the signing of the Arusha Accords in August 1993. It was agreed that the Rwanda Government, RPF, and other opposition party would all share power in the government at the end of which, there would be a democratic election. It was also agreed to establish a demilitarized zone in the northern part that was occupied by RPF, where no military could enter.

Following Arusha Accords, a ceasefire was followed. RPF delegates were sent to Kigali to participate in the transition national assembly with 600 RPF troops deployed in Kigali for their protection along with 2,500 soldiers of the peacekeeping force, the United Nations Assistance Mission for Rwanda (UNAMIR). UNAMIR was sent to the country to make sure the peace agreement is observed. This caused great consternation among Rwandans – bringing rebel troops within a sovereign nation was unheard of before. The RPF officials were housed at Conseil National de Development (CND) which is Rwanda's Parliament building, nearby my sister Jeanne Françoise Nakure's house.

With the arrival of RPF in Kigali, every patriot's antenna went up, especially those who have witnessed or heard of their atrocities. We wondered why those RPF officials could not be protected by the U.N. instead but brought their own select soldiers. Can you imagine a sovereign nation allowing an army of a rebel's movement to come inside their country with their own army? With their own weapons? RPF became even more strange when they said they would not eat the food from Kigali, nor use their water, but they would bring their own water and other goods from the Northern Part that they occupied.

We saw their big trucks going back and forth every day. It was said that instead of just bringing goods, they also brought weapons.

RPF trucks began to pour into Kigali, under the pretense of bringing food, water, and provisions for their officials and army, while instead they were bringing trucks full of weapons. Their trucks would not stop at the roadblocks where U.N. peacekeeping forces checked everything that entered the country through a demilitarized zone. Not only this, but RPF violated the accords, had their presence in the demilitarized zone, and they continued to kill people. They did not follow the ceasefire, but they took that occasion to strengthen their presence and power in the CND.

The Killing of Fidele Rwambuka, a Citizen Loved by All

In August the same year, Fidèle Rwambuka[10], the mayor of Kanzenze commune and member of the Central Committee of the then-ruling party, MRND, was also murdered at his home the night of August 25, 1993. Rwambuka was a great public servant. I knew this family. They were great citizens held in high esteem by many. In the night of August 25th, RPF shot Rwambuka dead, simply because he was a Hutu with influence. This dear man was deeply loved in the country and his killing was another way to fuel hatred towards Tutsis. Rwandans wondered how in the world one can support such rebels. Whatever Kagame did, it surely must have given him his heart's desire but it only fueled hatred towards Tutsi.

Attacks by shootings, bombs, grenades, and landmines continued throughout 1993. When the killings took place, Kagame's RPF denied it, but those who were in the country and had eyes to see, we know that it was done by the RPF. Even today, Kagame's RPF and DMI continues to kill and deny even when there is tangible proof. They worked so well with the international community to hide their killings, and to point fingers against the innocents who have no lobbyists and who do not lie. They worked by intrigue and deceit on a higher realm. RPF succeeded so well in this and buried the truth. So it was those barbaric acts that led some people to grow their hatred towards Tutsis. Kagame did everything he could to provoke Hutus to the maximum, and he won.

Kagame did not just want to negotiate and get a few seats in congress, he wanted it all. Kagame only cared for power so he could not be questioned by anyone. He did not care about anyone who was inside, whether Hutus or Tutsis... all he cared about was power.

6

RWANDA GENOCIDE AS I EXPERIENCED IT
APRIL 6, 1994 – JULY 7, 1994

MY SISTER JEANNE FRANÇOISE NAKURE

Jeanne Françoise Nakure was my senior sister by two years. It was April 1994, and by this time I was a freshman at Rwanda University. I left the university for two weeks break to visit Nakure. She was married to a handsome man, Jean Marie Vianney – he was an agriculture engineer and worked for an American organization under USAID. Nakure, on the other hand, worked as a Secretary for Rwanda's Minister of Public Affairs, Alexandre Muterahejuru.

I got to her house on April 5, 1994, and by this time, the war in Rwanda was at its worst. RPF had already created a climate of killings. Fear and tension between Hutus and Tutsis increased. That week would become the fateful week on Rwanda's calendar because it was during this week that the 1994 genocide took place.

Nakure and Jean Marie Vianney were newly married and

had their firstborn child, whom we nicknamed Bambine. They lived very close to the CND building where RPF officials stayed with their 600 soldiers. I remember being at my sister's during that fateful week, not knowing that in a few more hours I will see her no more. Truly, our time is in God's hand. He alone knows our last day on earth. It is good to live prepared and ready all the time, as if each day is our last day on the earth. That afternoon, Nakure, her sister-in-law, Cecilia, and I had a great visit. I remember how we decided to sing, each taking turns to sing a beautiful song. I remember Cecilia's song, it truly moved our hearts:

"*One day I had a dream*
I dreamt that the world was transformed
I saw the poor becoming rich
The broken being restored
Everyone being content"

From my sister's house we would look up at the sky and feel like there is something strange and unknown that was about to take place in Rwanda, but we could not put our finger on it. "What is it, oh, dear Lord?" we wondered. The afternoon of April 5th was unlike anything I had ever known in my life. The sky had a red tinge and the atmosphere was oppressive. Something was going to happen, but what?

As we visited, we would look at the CND building, that

horrible building where the murderers of my sister had a list of people to kill, and we had no idea. Unlike what Kagame told the world, Rwandans did not have a list because they did not plan to shut down the plane that carried the president, and that is the root that sparked the genocide.

Rwandans did not plan to kill anyone. Rwandans did not like wars, and they did not start a war. Kagame was a man of war. In Uganda he had fought alongside Museveni and he had become the head of the Military Intelligence of Uganda. In Uganda, Paul Kagame was known as Pilato (after Pontius Pilate) because Ugandans realized that he was a sadistic killer and torturer. While the international community was told that Rwandans had lists of people to kill, and had dug holes prior to genocide, they were lies. This is a bogus story Kagame made up and he was successful at it because he took advantage of Rwandans' innocence. They trusted everyone, including him.

Visiting at my sister's house, act times, we would be wondering about our tomorrow. For sure it was very uncertain. We had a great girly time, visiting and playing with our little niece Bambine. She would have been about six months old or so at the time. Before the day ended, Cecilia went to her home. Her father was an accomplished lawyer, but he was a widow. Cecile's mom had died years before the genocide. After Cecilia left, I planned to stay at Nakure's house for two more weeks before heading back to school.

My Sister Taken and Killed, Hours After I left Her Home

April 6, 1994, for me, will always be known as "The Cursed Day." Nakure had to go to work. I snatched a few hours of conversation with her before she left. I stayed with Bambine and the maid who took care of her. I remember that during the day, I even talked to Nakure on the phone. From her workplace, she would call to check on Bambine.

She had a full-time maid, who was also a relative, Manirakiza. The original plan was for me to stay until the two weeks were over, but before evening came I had changed my mind about staying. I felt pushed by something inside me to go to the hill country where my parents had a farm, and where my grandparents lived. At this time, my younger siblings were also there. We had been orphaned about 10 years earlier. Both my father and mother died within the same year.

My sister and her husband could not understand why I changed my mind so quickly because I had planned to stay with them in Kigali. That day, I talked to both of them, and they tried to convince me to stay. We argued without agreeing and finally, I left, promising to come back again. I gave a big kiss to Bambine and left. But we did not know this was all the plan of The Almighty God who wanted me to survive what was coming that night!

Within hours after leaving their home, they became victims of the Rwanda genocide. I never saw them again but worse, today the government of Rwanda does not allow Hutus to commemorate the genocide, so those who are inside the country cannot officially mourn her. The only commemoration they have is for the genocide against Tutsi. Anyone who raises this issue is charged with genocide ideology, and at times as a genocidaire.

Kagame's regime threatens anyone who has questions about the genocide. So, Hutus, who lost their own people, only commemorate the genocide against Tutsis. In Rwanda, it is perceived as a crime to argue on this subject, though RPF killed thousands of people during the genocide. (Please read the book "*In Praise of Blood: The crimes of the Rwandan Patriotic Front*" to gain a better understanding of the role of RPF in the genocide.)

When I changed my mind about staying, I called my brother, Dirimasi Jean Damascene, to ask if he would drop me off at our home in Rushashi, in the countryside where we also had a farm. Rushashi was a distance of about 32 miles from Kigali. He agreed, came, and drove me to the country where he also had to pick up his little boy who was visiting with his uncles and great grandparents.

I had a great time visiting with my brother while driving to the hill country. I love my brother so much because he gave his all to raise us after losing our parents. But, like Nakure, I did not know that something bad was going to happen to my brother, that would cause him to be unjustly imprisoned for 13 years in Rwanda. Yes, at the end of the genocide, Kagame came full of wrath and threw Hutus in jail who were well off. My beloved brother was thrown in jail in 1995 for 13 years. His only crime was that he was an educated rich Hutu.

My two younger sisters, Chantal and Assoumpta, were already in the hill country for Easter break. My three brothers, Regis, Pascal, and Philbert were also waiting for me, but Damascene had to go back to the city to join his family. He was already married, and they had three young boys.

We grew up as a close family, a family of many children. We partied together and we supported each other. There was, therefore, such an excitement when I arrived to the countryside, to see one another again after three months of being away, but especially everyone wanted to hear about my first year at the university. We were looking forward to having so much fun together that we threw a party for ourselves and started to celebrate. A goat was killed and there was an abundance of food. They had planned it to be a great celebration, and it was indeed – in the beginning!

Celebration Turns into Tragedy

No sooner had we started to celebrate, than this party turned into a tragedy. Quickly, as we were listening to the evening news from the national radio, we heard that the plane of Rwanda President Habyarimana Juvenal had been shot down while he was on his way from Tanzania. He had gone to sign the pact of peace with Kagame and RPF who were at war with Rwanda. Our president was killed at once, but also the President of Burundi who was with him as well as some other members of their cabinets. The most important people in the cabinet, from both Rwanda and Burundi, were dead!

The President of Rwanda was loved very much by the majority of Hutus inside the country and they believed that he had been killed by none other than Kagame. It was said that Kagame had boasted many times that he would finish him. Many people knew that the President's death would be followed by something bad, including the shedding of lots of innocent blood because an indescribable hatred had been growing between those two tribes and they had been fighting for power since 1990.

Nobody had doubt as to who would have brought this plane down, because nobody was killed in Rwanda until RPF came. We Rwandans who lived inside the country know who the killers were since the time of war. We Rwandans who lived inside knew who brought the barbaric culture of torturing, kidnapping, and killing. That one man was none other than Kagame himself.

But one thing we could not understand was, how can you kill someone who has agreed to sit at the negotiation table with you? How can you kill them on their way back from meeting with you, and signing a peace treaty with you? It was beyond Rwandans' understanding!

THE NIGHT TWO PRESIDENTS WERE ASSASSINATED

It was in the news, and read, "In the night of 6th April 1994 the presidential jet that carried President HABYARIMANA Juvenal was hit by a missile as it prepared to land at Kigali International Airport known then as Gregoire Kayibanda International Airport. Habyarimana along with eleven passengers aboard the plane did not survive the attack. The eleven passengers are Cyprien NTARYAMIRA, President of Burundi, Bernard CIZA, Burundi's Minister of Public Works, Cyriaque SIMBIZI, Burundi's Minister of Communication, Major General Déogratias NSABIMANA, Chief of Staff of the Rwandan Army, Major Thaddée BAGARAGAZA, responsible for the "maison militaire" of the Rwandan president, Colonel Elie SAGATWA, Member of the special secretariat of the Rwandan president, Chief of the Military Cabinet of the Rwandan president, Juvénal RENZAHO, foreign affairs advisor to the Rwandan president, Dr Emmanuel AKINGENEYE, personal physician to the Rwandan president and three French aircraft crew: Jacky HERAUD (pilot) Jean-Pierre MINABERRY (co-pilot) and Jean-Michel PERRINE (flight engineer)" [1].

The killing of President Habyarimana not only sparked other political assassinations but it also provoked and triggered the genocide.

It is said that Habyarimana's assassination is one of the sixteen most recognized political assassination in the last half-century, such as the assassination of the Kennedy brothers and Martin Luther King in the United States, Lord Mountbatten in Europe, and Indira Gandhi in Asia. [2]

RWANDA GENOCIDE 1994:
KILLINGS IN REMERA BY RPF

After hearing the news about the President's death, my first thoughts went to Nakure and her family. They were living in the capital city where roads were immediately closed so that no one could enter nor get out of the city. They were living in Remera, in the neighborhood of CND, where RPF officers and their 600 soldiers were housed. These people were not afraid to kill, and I was concerned deeply about my sister.

Indeed, immediately after the shooting down of the presidential airplane, RPF military forces took control of the neighborhood where my sister lived. They had spied on the neighborhood and knew the households of prominent-educated Hutus' families.

On April 7th, before the real genocide happens, the RPF busted through their metallic gate, they talked to the husband at first, and obliged him to have his family follow them. They checked the whole house to make sure nobody was left there. When they entered the house, there was a picture of President Ndadaye of Burundi, a Hutu president who had just been killed a few months earlier. He was the first democratically elected and first Hutu president of Burundi after winning the landmark 1993 election but was assassinated by Tutsi officers. Ndadaye was the most loved president and at the time, his portrait was a best seller in Rwanda.

My sister happened to have one hanging in her house. The RPF Tutsi soldiers commented on the picture and to them that was a great crime enough to kill the family. Vianney, Nakure, baby Bambine and Manirakiza the teenage maid were all terrified knowing they are in the hands of RPF. Besides the maid, they had also a cook who went to hide in the toilet that was on the outside and luckily, they did not check there. This cook survived and he is the one who told us what happened to our beloved family.

For this, I give thanks to God who has allowed this witness to survive so that we can know what happened to our dearest family.

Nakure and her family were then taken in inhuman ways, being kicked and led like animals to slaughter. My sister had a recent accident, and had been on crutches for some time. Her ankle was broken, so they dragged her to the Remera Stadium where thousands of people were rounded up. The UNAMIR peacekeepers were present to try and help over 30,000 refugees in there. This is where my sister Nakure and her husband were taken. For days, there was no food. A story was told us that even when the food finally came, there was no utensil, no plates no cup, people were using their shoes as plates.

My sister along with her entire family were killed by the RPF soldiers who controlled the area. Per their ID, my sister and her family were identified as Hutus. Educated Hutus was something RPF would not tolerate, and my sister was killed alongside her family. A report from Human Right Watch said, "*A number of people who had taken refuge under UNAMIR protection at Amahoro stadium were taken away by RPF soldiers and then "disappeared." Among them were Charles Ngendahimana, younger brother of the assassinated politician Emmanuel Gapyisi, and Doctor Prudence, a physician who had been treating the injured and wounded in the stadium.*"[3] Most of the prominent Hutus in the area near Remera and by CND did not escape these killings by the RPF.

Pauline Kayitesi has shared her testimony of the killings

in this area of Remera near CND[4]. I know the family of Kayitesi. Her two sisters, Claudine and Didier, and I went to the same school. They were the most intelligent and well-behaved young ladies you would ever see. Both were leaders. Kayitesi said she survived because she was in Europe at the time. Kayitesi reports that on April 7, 1994, when even the genocide against Tutsis had not officially started, Kagame's RPF army came with a list of Hutus that were to be killed. RPF then murdered her father, three brothers, and Didier. "All those who were at home had been killed." The family members who were still alive only survived "because they were not at home." The servant in this family survived to tell the story.

Kayitesi parents were killed because they were educated Hutus. In the Remera suburb where her family lived, barely any Hutus escaped. Today in Rwanda, it is recognized as the genocide against Tutsi. In Rwanda Kayitesi has no room to mourn her family.

None of these killings and massacres would have happened if the plane of president Habyarimana had not been shot down. The genocide would not have happened if the assassination of these two presidents had not happened. To solve the Rwanda problems, one has to go back to the source where everything began. To seek to move forward without dealing with the root problem would be like a doctor curing the symptoms rather than the root cause of the sickness. A thorough investigation into the assassination of president Habyarimana is of the essence.

Death of Cecilia

Cecilia and I were the same age. She worked not too far from CND. During the girly talk, she had mentioned how she was dating an RPF soldier. When I heard about that, my antenna went up, and now I know that my instinct was right in warning me.

Her parents' home was nearby Kanombe airport where the presidential airplane was shot down. RPF controlled this area. The so-called boyfriend was on a mission to destroy her. When the genocide happened, the boyfriend came to take possession of the very nice home that Cecilia's family owned. He decided to kill her hoping the rest would find death somewhere else. Cecilia was thrown alive in the latrine. Neighbors that survived these atrocities reported that in their hiding place, for three days they heard her screams coming from the outside toilet. Nobody came to her help. She died this horrible death.

The story of Cecilia, Pauline Kayitesi, and Nakure, shows you that during the Rwanda genocide, Hutus were also murdered by RPF. In every territory that was controlled by the RPF, thousands upon thousands of Hutus, and even some Tutsis, died by the hand of the RPF.

'Genocide Against Tutsi' Is the Official Narrative

Isn't this a problem today, that there is only one official narrative of the Rwanda genocide? It is the narrative given by Kagame. It is the narrative given by those who also committed great atrocities. The narrative of the ones who brought down the plane carrying two presidents. Rwanda pushed and lobbied aggressively for a U.N. resolution to designate a day of memory for the country's genocide, specifically against the Tutsi ethnic group, supporting a move widely seen as downplaying the deaths of thousands of Hutus during the 1994 civil war. The resolution was opposed by the U.S. and European countries, but it won support from Israel.[5]

The resolution passed and it renamed the "International Day of Reflection on the 1994 Genocide in Rwanda," marked on April 7, as "International Day of Reflection on 1994 Genocide against Tutsi in Rwanda" so this helped Kagame and his RPF to cover up their own crimes. After killing and winning this war, Kagame and the RPF took control of the country and began to reign. They enacted severe laws governing the genocide. Anyone inside Rwanda who would call this day as "genocide" was perceived as an enemy to the country.

Today in Paul Kagame's Rwanda, anyone who asks about Hutus being killed during the genocide, anyone who would raise a question about genocide, would be seen as a genocidaire or a genocide denier. There are thousands of people who have been imprisoned and murdered, accused of genocide ideology.

Kizito Mihigo, the Rwanda artist and Tutsi survivor was imprisoned and murdered for fighting for the rights of Hutus to be remembered during the genocide commemoration. As I told you, before his death, he recorded himself and sent this message overseas, asking that it would be played only if he were to be murdered. Channel 4 TV played this message on February 21, 2020, and it said,

"Rwanda is an open-air prison.

Each time you bring up the subject of other victims,

the people who were killed by the RPF,

you are labeled a genocide denier."

REJECTING UN INTERVENTION FORCE DURING THE GENOCIDE: KAGAME SAID IT WAS TOO LATE TO STOP GENOCIDE.

Statement by the RPF on the proposed deployment of a U.N. intervention force in Rwanda on April 30, 1994[6]

Kagame did not just want to negotiate. While the signing of Arusha Accords were viewed by political parties in the opposition as a big win, for Kagame it was defeat. This is because all Kagame cared for was the power where he could not be questioned by anyone. He did not care about anyone who was inside Rwanda, whether Hutus or Tutsis. All he cared for was power. This is why, after signing the accords, he turned around and brought down two presidents who were elected by their citizens.

May 12, 1994, 24 days into the genocide, the U.N. offered to send intervention to Rwanda to stop the genocide. Kagame, who was leading the RPF army, responded that the time for U.N. intervention is long past. "The genocide is almost completed. Most of the potential victims of the regime have either been killed or have since fled."

These are Kagame's own words: "We are only opposed to what they call the U.N. Intervention Force, because we felt it was irrelevant in the circumstances. We did not understand what that intervention would serve as a purpose, when genocide has been carried in this country almost with impunity, and when it's near completion, then people talk about intervention."

Himbara wrote, "Kagame's RPF had already rejected the U.N. Intervention Force. On April 30, 1994, the RPF informed the U.N. Security Council that 'the Rwandese Patriotic Front hereby declares that it is categorically opposed to the proposed U.N. Intervention Force and will not under any circumstances cooperate with its setting up or operation.'"[7]

Genocide began on April 7, 1994. On April 30, 1994, when Kagame's RPF was rejecting the U.N. Intervention Force, genocide was only 23 days old. But to Paul Kagame, it was too late for the outside world to intervene. In his own words, genocide was "near completion." But of course, as we now know, genocide took more lives in the rest of April, May, June, and July, 1994. Kagame was not interested in saving lives. He was interested in capturing power."

RWANDA GENOCIDE 1994: KILLINGS AT RWANKUBA PARISH BY INTERAHAMWE

In the countryside where my brother had dropped me, days went by without hearing the whereabouts of our loved ones who were in Kigali. Long were the days, long were the nights, where we hoped to hear from Jean Damascene and Nakure in vain. The RPF knew in advance what would happen after shooting down the presidential plane. Therefore, they began killings right afterward, even before the genocide committed by Hutus began.

Life during the first week of the genocide was quiet in the countryside. Day in and day out, however, we began to hear bombs from a very long distance. In the countryside, the killings had not yet begun. People continued their lives as normal: waking up early in the morning, going to the fields with hoes, and cultivating the land. Coffee, banana trees, Irish potatoes, beans, corn, and vegetables is what you could mainly see in the field. It is a true lush and green country of a thousand hills. The weather is tropical, which does not change much throughout the year. People went by to walk in the fields and do different activities. At evening time, people gathered to listen to the national news. There was only one main station, but RPF had also begun to broadcast since the war. Listening to the news through national radio was almost the only way to know what was going on during this time, besides people transmitting information orally.

The genocide in Rushashi did not start until May or so. Being a Catholic at the time, like almost everyone I knew, we went to the mass at Rwankuba Catholic parish on this particular Sunday. The Mass was not yet over when all of sudden we saw the head nun standing up and leaving quickly after whispering to the nun who was sitting next to her. This was unusual for the head nun to leave before the mass was over.

After her departure, other nuns proceeded towards the exit and they left the church building quietly. One by one they left the church. Inside the church building, one could easily see new faces, but we did not understand what was going on. At home, none of us had a clue that people will truly kill. After the mass was over, we learned from the people outside that the new faces were Tutsis who, after hearing about the death of President Habyarimana, knew there would be killings against them, and they had taken refuge at Rwankuba parish, leaving their homes and their belongings behind. There were some Tutsis among the nuns as well.

In Rushashi commune, especially at Rwankuba parish, there used to be unity in the community. There were very few Tutsi families in this community, and you could easily count them on one hand. The killings were to start among those who had taken refuge at the church, and very soon we saw that it spread to mostly Tutsi who were non-native of the area. As for my family, God's hand rested upon us. We were a mixed family of Hutus and Tutsis, in the beginning we only received threats. We were also lucky that we were in central Rwanda which was not controlled yet by the RPF.

While the service was still going on, I was physically sitting inside this church, but my mind was a million miles away. Why were these killings going on, and what was going to be the end of all these things? Was there any existing force that could stand against what was to take place? It seemed like the gates of hell were unleashed over the nation, and that no matter what we tried to help or stop, it was beyond what helpless divided society could do. Very soon I found out that fear, greed, and the spirit of murder were ruling in Rwanda and influencing the whole atmosphere.

I don't remember much about what happened during the service, but I remember hearing lots of noise coming from outside the church. Alas, it was a mob that was outside, having come to kill, steal, and destroy.

As the service dismissed, we left. Parish doors and the gates to the monastery were locked and only those who had taken refuge in the parish days before were allowed to stay inside. Outside the parish building stood a mob of about 50 people with swords, knives, machetes, and traditional weapons in their hands. I glanced through them and I was only to recognize one kid who was a school dropout. I did not see any leaders of the people like Bourgmestre or cell leaders. I only saw the gangs. I only saw wicked people, not normal people. I did not see anyone with education partaking in the killings but the opportunists, the thieves, the robbers, the school dropouts – those are the people I remember seeing who came to kill.

They stood there, eyes looking at everyone coming outside the church sanctuary. Those people's faces had a devilish countenance, ready to drink the blood of many innocent lives.

There was no time to lose. I went to find my young siblings and we quickly left to go home. My younger sister recognized one person among the mob, whom she tried to greet but received a threat, "We can kill you too, we are not afraid!"

Unlike other Sundays, when we would normally hang around at Rwankuba's shopping center known as Rwandago, this time we left quickly to go home and see what we could do to survive the days ahead.

That Sunday afternoon, we all sat in Bigabiro Hills where we had a nice home and a nice view on the top of the mountain.

From a long distance, we heard that the mob started singing a slogan. Later on, we heard from neighbors who went close by that this mob requested the white missionary priest to give over the people who had taken refuge inside the parish, telling the priest that they would kill them and leave the parish without damaging it. If the priest refused, they would use force to get in. The priest who had read the mass would not give over the lives of those people. He refused.

The mob did not try to negotiate. They very soon started throwing rocks at the stained-glass windows. The parish's many buildings were attacked. The mob had many people joining in, little by little. These were the ones attracted by the riches of this world. They were driven by the anger and rage from the killing of their president but also by the idea that they would get to loot the parish and take the belongings of those whom they killed. Evil power was given to those who agreed to kill—they would very soon kill the young and the old. They had neither compassion, nor pity, on the poor or rich, nor on the weak or the strong.

The mob started throwing rocks at the parish doors, at the windows, and everywhere they could, making noises that were heard everywhere in the surrounding region. They broke windows and tried to force their way in. They were not successful until they spotted a car carrying another priest who was coming from saying a mass at another sub-parish church. When the priest's car was let in, the mob seized that moment and rushed inside the gate like hungry lions. They rushed towards those who had come to seek refuge and started killing them with knives and machetes, taking all of their belongings. They would run home to deposit what they looted and run back to where the killings were taking place to kill more and loot more.

From April 1994 to July 1994, lots of individuals died in the mass killings that took place throughout the country. These were the most perilous months, ever, in the history of Rwanda. I remember those days when some houses and some churches were burned with people inside. I remember those days when children, whose parents had been massacred, were left alone, living days and nights in the parish cemetery without anyone to care for them. In those days, some of the killers were creative in their evil ways of tormenting the people, and before people were killed, they would be given only two choices: either to dig their graves before being killed or to be killed and never be buried. I remember those days when we spent days in hiding, when I lost many family members and best friends. Days when sin increased more and more and ruled in the whole country.

There was no place to hide from these killings. It seemed as if the devil himself was ruling in Rwanda. Those killings reached every corner, every family. People met death at every turn. Those killings divided people and families and broke up marriages and best friends. Sorrow and gloom could be seen everywhere during that time. There were signs of devastation in the sky and everywhere you looked. We were surrounded by uncertainty. "What was going to be the end of all the evil that was happening? Was there any hope," we wondered.

The cry of distress over the loss of so many lives was everywhere. In Rushashi, there were not many Tutsis, so the killings took a little while, but the war increased and every day, it got closer to us. Food became scarce and life became about survival. We were to eat only once a day, and we even thought about eating every other day.

In the midst of all of this, in the middle of one night, I had a dream that Rwanda will not win the war. From that dream, I talked to my siblings and other family members and we knew that we had to flee to another country. I, like many other people, knew who Kagame was. He is the guy who taught Rwandans how to kill, he is the guy who provoked tribes into killing each other so that he can get the power. We knew that he is not coming to Rwanda to establish democracy. This is why, when he took the country, thousands upon thousands of citizens fled the country.

7

RPF HOSTILITY TOWARDS CHRISTIANITY & THE CATHOLIC CHURCH

In one day, Three Bishops, Nine Priests, One Brother And Two Civilians Brutally Murdered (06-05-1994)

"Blessed are those who have been persecuted for the sake of righteousness, for theirs is the kingdom of heaven."

Matthew 5:10

RWANDA GENOCIDE 1994: THE KILLINGS OF CLERGY AT GAKURAZO BY KAGAME'S RPF

The following testimony[1] is brought to us by a dear friend of mine, Madame Espérance Mukashema – a true human rights activist, a defender of truth, and a freedom fighter. She is a Tutsi survivor of the 1994 Rwanda genocide. She has now fled Rwanda and lives in the Netherlands where she continues to speak up about the atrocities committed by Kagame and his RPF from the time of 1994 genocide up to now. She is a journalist and also the host of Radio Ubumwe and author of the book "They Killed an Angel, My Last Born Son Richard Sheja." Espérance can be reached via WhatsApp +31 6 84941329.

On June 5th of 1994, in Gakurazo, Bishop Joseph Ruzindana of Byumba (North), Bishop Thaddée Nsengiyumva of Kabgayi (Center), Archbishop Vincent Nsengiyumva of Kigali, who was also the President of the Conference of Catholic Bishops of Rwanda, and several other religious leaders were murdered. Mukashema, who is an eyewitness and was present during the brutal murder of these religious leaders, brings us her unprecedented testimony.

Not only does she explain in detail the unfolding of this atrocity, but, also, she claims to hold the evidence that the orders to exterminate members of the Clergy came directly from Paul Kagame, the current President of Rwanda. Mukashema is a Tutsi survivor who first fled Rwanda under the dictatorship of Kagame to Uganda in 2000 for three years before settling in the Netherlands.

On this terrible day of June 5, 1994, Mukashema was present in Gakurazo when several people, including three bishops, nine priests, one Brother and two civilians were savagely murdered by the Rwandan Patriotic Front (RPF). During these massacres, Richard Sheja, an eight-year-old boy, who is also the son of Mukashema was among those killed.

Picture of Some Rwanda Bishops in 1994

Transfer of Clerics from Kabgayi Dioceses to Gakurazo Before the Killings

It all started on June 2nd, 1994, reported Mukashema, "When the RPF 157 battalion led by Colonel Fred Ibingira (Today an RPF General) besieged Kabgayi diocese. The latter decided shortly afterward to move refugees who had settled there. Half of the refugees were transferred to Ruhango, including the murdered clergy men, and another half was brought to Gakurazo, in a novitiate of the Jesuit Brothers led by a Burundian, Brother Balthazar. Three days later, on June 5, 1994, the clergy were again transferred, this time from Ruhango to Gakurazo,"

161

She also said that a group of clerics, including three bishops, arrived under an RPF escort around 11:00 am in Gakurazo. "We welcomed them," she said. "I even remember that Bishop Nsengiyumva of Kigali said a mass in the chapel because that day was Pentecost. When these clergymen arrived in Gakurazo, I had been there for three months. Those who were there were mostly Tutsi refugees, but there were also some Hutus. I lived in room number four. Brother Balthazar asked me to give my room to Bishop Nsengiyumva. I was placed in a general dormitory together with other refugees. I was with three of my children, Sheja, Gaju, and Shema. My husband had been murdered earlier during the genocide on April 28, 1994. He was murdered near Nyanza in a place called Gasoro,"

Massacres at Dusk

In her story, Mukashema goes on to say that the clerics were murdered the very day of their arrival. Thus, "At Gakurazo, the same day of June 5th, 1994, around 7:00 pm, a soldier named Wilson Ukwishaka came to brother Balthazar and said, "Please gather all the people which came this morning. We are going to have a meeting with them." He did not solicit all the refugees who were there. He made it clear that only the refugees who had arrived from Ruhango had to report to the refectory for a meeting.

Brother Balthazar went to gather all of them. At that time, Bishop of Kigali Nsengiyumva was in his room. Everyone came to the refectory. I was there, too, sitting on a bench in the back, and I was with one of my children. There were people setting up the tables because it was dinner time. Next to me was Bishop Gasabwoya, who held on his knees my eldest son who was eight years old.

When everyone had finished settling, Wilson said only these words: "We just took the country, we are in control of all this area, I will talk with you about how we can work together." These are the only words I heard from him. My youngest son who was about four years old was not feeling well, so I took him out. Arriving at the door, a young soldier who was there asked me to go back and take my other child who had stayed with the bishop. I did not know why he was asking me that, so I went back into the room to pick him up. But Bishop Gasabwoya insisted, "Why do you want to take this child when he seems to get along well with me?" At that moment, the soldier who had advised me to pick up the child rushed in and pushed away the girls who served the meal, he pushed them all the way to the door. I too quickly left, leaving my son with Bishop Gasabwoya. Arriving at the door, I saw several soldiers coming in rushing, running, and several others entered through the windows. Immediately, without warning they began shooting!"

"I think the soldiers started shooting from one side because

I heard my son screaming loudly, calling me, he thought maybe I could save him. I heard him shout 'Mom, Mom,' and because the door was open, I could hear him. At that moment, they killed everyone, the bodies were laying everywhere, on the ground, everywhere. Hearing the gunshots, people from outside got scattered everywhere; some went to hide in the showers, others went out of the novitiate. I remained paralyzed for a few seconds in front of the door, not knowing what to do. Then I regained my senses and went to hide in the bathroom with the child I had in my arms. I felt pain that I do not know how to express."

Murders Attributed to an Imaginary Maniac

Mukashema explained how the killers she saw tried to fool people and attribute their wicked deeds to a mad ghost. "Shortly after the shooting had stopped, they whistled and gathered us on the ground. There was this Wilson and several other soldiers whose names I do not remember," Mukashema recalls. "I would like to tell you that a misfortune just happened. There is a young man who has entered the refectory; he has murdered the people, and has subsequently committed suicide. Come, I will go ahead of you and show you where his body is lying," said Wilson.

He had a flashlight in his hands because at that moment electricity was cut off. He brought us behind the chapel, and showed us something lying on the ground, covered by many clothes. He told us, "Here is the person who murdered these people, and who subsequently committed suicide." It was hard to tell if it was a man. All we could see was a pile of clothes covering an object that could not be identified. He did not take off the clothes to show us the person himself, he did not even say who it was," Mukashema said.

"Shut up, or the Rest of Your Children Will Become Orphans"

In her story, Mukashema goes on to say how she was forced to remain silent about the death of her son. "Suffering in anonymity was my only option to save my life. I had just lost my husband and eldest son in a span of three months," she said. "We spent the night there. In the morning a lot of people arrived, even General Ibingira (Colonel at that time).

The military went everywhere. I was angry to the point of beginning to call them and treat the RPF's as Interahamwe (terrorists). It was at that moment that a person approached me and said, 'You treat them as Interahamwe? Do you want your remaining children to become orphans? It seems like you have not yet understood who these RPF are, and how they work? I advise you to shut up and remain calm. If you continue to treat them as Interahamwe, you will die and your remaining children will become orphans," she said.

A Burial Worthy of Animals

"After the barbaric assassination of the clergy and those who accompanied them, the victims were entitled to an animal-worthy burial from their executioners," said Mukashema. "They dug a common grave behind the novitiate, and all the dead were thrown in there, buried like worthless animals. My son's body was there, I touched him, and even said goodbye. After that, life continued. We stayed there until the arrival of the French soldiers of Operation Turquoise who evacuated us, and brought us to another, more secure site."

One of the Executioners Turned Diplomat

Mukashema points to General Innocent Kabandana as one of the brains behind these assassinations in Gakurazo. Within the RPF, Kabanda's assignments have always been spying and intelligence." Among the people who came to pick us up, there was Kabandana who, until the publishing of the testimony, was Chargé d'affaires at the Rwandan embassy in the United States. He was transferred back to Rwanda shortly after the public release of this testimony," Mukashema reported.

"This Kabandana was also part of the group that brought the bishops on June 5, 1994. Back then, he was a lieutenant and was one of the people whom we called 'the psis.' These were the people who organized RPF meetings. Kabandana was involved in making all the decisions; he could not be ignorant of this murderous plan. He was actively involved," confirmed Mukashema. She also testified that the killings of refugees who had settled in Gakurazo continued elsewhere they settled, in order to remove potential witnesses.

"When we left Gitarama, many were transferred to Kinazi. I was among the group that was transferred to Bugesera, nevertheless I followed closely the news of the people who had been transported to Kinazi. That's how I learned that when he arrived in Kinazi, brother Balthazar, who also helped so many refugees at Gakurazo, was murdered on the spot together with Vivens, who was the younger brother of Bishop Kalibushi of Gisenyi," tells Mukashema.

She wrote a letter to one of the U.S. ministers, asking for the arrest of Kabandana, who in her eyes is one of her son's killers. "I do not understand how an assassin can go to represent Rwanda in the United States, as if, among millions of Rwandans, there are no respectful people who can do this job," Mukashema said in denouncement of him. "A diplomat must be a person above reproach. The one I denounce today is Kabandana, the diplomat who is currently on American soil after murdering my son.

"A Credible Eyewitness … I would Never Have Been Safe in Rwanda"

Mukashema continues to tell her amazing testimony[1]. As a personal friend, Mukashema has given me permission for the writing of her story to be included, so that the whole world will know the truth that has been hidden for so long.

Mukashema says that she was forced to flee Rwanda in 2000, because the threat hovered over her due to what she had seen and heard. "I left Rwanda in the year 2000. People told me that General Ibingira had killed my people, and that he was involved in several other massacres. Since I am a credible witness against the ignominies of this General, I would never have been safe in Rwanda," she said. "It's true that I felt danger everywhere. I cannot tell everything here, but all I can say is that I was seriously in danger. The RPF government always gets rid of anyone who knows more about their atrocities."

She further claimed that the massacres at Gakurazo were in no way a reprisal for some Tutsi who were avenging their murdered families, because among the slaughtered people there were many Tutsi, such as Bishop Joseph Ruzindana of Byumba; Father Denis Mutabazi of the Diocese of Nyundo; Brother Jean Baptiste Nsinga, Superior General of the Joséphist Brothers, Fr. François Xavier Muligo the priest of the Kabgayi Cathedral, and more.

"The Order to Slaughter the Clergymen Came Directly From General Paul Kagame"

According to Mukashema, the religious leaders were not killed by the people of Rwanda, but by RPF on the direct orders of Paul Kagame, the current strongman of Rwanda. "I saw everything. Even after the assassination, I conducted my little investigation and questioned a lot of people," she said, adding, "There are many details that I cannot communicate here. It is the business of justice. Currently, there is no justice in Rwanda, but when justice time arrives, I will put at the disposal of the investigators all that I know. But to quell the curiosity, I can tell you that the massacres were perpetrated by RPF – the rebel group from Uganda, who were personally seeking to eliminate the three bishops. However, to erase any evidence, they murdered everyone in the room. I was told personally that Ibingira contacted Kagame by radio to warn him that there was a child in the room; Kagame ordered him to "kill everyone."

Mukashema assured that killing the child was not a coincidence, but a calculation on the part of the executioners because "they wanted to fool people and make them believe that an enraged person entered the room, and killed everyone, even a child. The message was to deceive people and show that only a maniac can murder a child," she said. "I cannot reveal to you the person who told me that the order to kill everyone came from

Paul Kagame, but when the time of justice arrives, that person will be known, and she is ready to testify. They were talking to each other (Paul Kagame and Ibingira) by walkie talkie, so the witness heard Ibingira say, "There is a child." She also heard Kagame reply, "Kill everyone."

"What I have said here are the things I witnessed with my very own eyes and heard with my own ears," says Mukashema. "This is not a testimony coming from a third party," she insisted.

Mock Trial – The Criminals Judging Themselves

As a reminder, in 2008 at the Military Court of Kigali, a "mock trial" took place, to try those responsible for the assassinations of clergymen in Gakurazo. However, the Kigali regime hastened to organize a trial, because the Arusha-based International Criminal Tribunal for Rwanda (ICTR) was beginning to take an interest in this case, following the pressure from the Human Rights Watch (HRW).

At the dock, Brigadier General Wilson Gumisiriza, Major Wilson Ukwishaka, and Captains John Butera and Dieudonné Rukeba, who were their subordinates in the 157th RPF battalion, were all accused of murdering the clergy at the time. General Wilson Gumisiriza and Major Wilson Ukwishaka were both acquitted. Yet Captain Kayijuka Ngabo, a military prosecutor, had requested life imprisonment for them. Captains John Butera and Dieudonne Rukeba each received eight years of jail time.

The ICTR prosecutor, Hassan Bubacar Jallow, had warned the day after the arrest of these officers, that Rwandan justice could be unsuccessful if the trial did not meet international standards in this area. Cameroonian William Egbe, charged by Jallow to follow up on this procedure, refused to give his assessment of the course of the trial. According to a source at the military prosecutor's office in Kigali, contacted by the Hirondelle Agency in October 2008, at each hearing, there was a representative of the Prosecutor's Office of the ICTR and all the information was brought to the attention of the Jallow team.

More Clergy Massacres by the RPF

The massacres of Gakurazo are neither the first, nor the last, massacres of the clergy perpetrated by the RPF. The RPF has always been anti-Christian. They are also accused of perpetrating several other massacres against clergy in Rwanda and Congo. In Rwanda, there have been for example the following clergy assassinations:

- In April 1994, nine priests were murdered at the Minor Seminary of Rwesero
- In April 1994, nine Spanish missionaries were massacred in Kibungo
- On October 17, 1994, Quebec priest Guy Simard, parish

priest of Ruyenzi (Butare) was murdered

- February 02, 1997, during a religious homily by Father Guy Pinard, parish priest of Kampanga (Ruhengeri) was shot dead
- On August 1, 1995, Father Pie Ntahobari, pastor of Kamonyi (Gitarama) was brutally murdered
- May 11, 1997, two priests from the parish of Cyahinda (Butare) were killed
- In August 1997, Father Ignace Mubashankwaya of Mushaka Parish (Cyangugu) was killed
- On January 31, 1998, in Kigali, Croatian father Vijeko Curic was killed
- On April 28, 1998, the parish priest Boniface Kagabo from Ruhengeri Parish was murdered
- On the night of January 7-8, 1998, six sisters of the Resurrection of Christ in Busasamana were massacred

Add to these assassinations, the disappearance in 1996 of Bishop Phocas Nikwigize of Ruhengeri, returning from the refugee camps in Eastern DRC (former Zaire); the imprisonment of Mgr. Augustin Misago and the death of Mgr. André Sibomana, who died after Kagame's regime refused him traveling documents to go for treatment abroad. In Congo, there was also the assassination of Bishop Christophe Munzihirwa on October 26, 1996, as well as the assassination of several dozen priests and nuns.

Closing Remarks

Who are these RPF people who have murdered countless Rwandans and many others. Never before in the history of Rwanda, has anyone ever had the audacity to murder in such manner; never before, has anyone disrespected the clergy!
These Rwandan bishops and priests were people of noble character. They were the fountain of wisdom in Rwanda. They were great, great people whom we respected. They were the 'think tank' of the Rwandan society. Destroying them was destroying all of us.

These innocent people were killed right before the end of the genocide! To this day, no justice has been applied to them. After they were killed, Kagame moved on, using the weapon of character assassination when talking to the West and to the Vatican, labeling them as genocidaire. He lobbied aggressively and the dead had no voice to speak except through you and me. Beloved reader, Rwanda has a big problem. Rwandans are facing a mountain that is bigger than they are. We ask each one of you to lead truth to victory.

Even today, some of the family members of the murdered clergy cannot mourn them, especially if they are Hutus. God in His providence has brought forth this book to let the whole world know that He has received many of them in His kingdom. They are in a beautiful country, far above their murderers. They are not dead, but have a real life. They truly live now. Through this book, let their voice be heard and let their justice come forth!

8

SURVIVING AND ESCAPE TO CONGO JULY 1994

The cords of death encompassed me, and the torrents of
ungodliness terrified me.
The cords of Sheol surrounded me; the snares of death
confronted me
In my distress I called upon the Lord, and cried to my God for help;
He heard my voice out of His temple
And my cry for help before Him came into His ears.
(Psalm 18:4-6)

Through many tears, dangers, loss of relatives, and the loss of almost everything, I came out of that genocide sound and alive. Following the dream, I fled to the to the neighboring country of Zaire/Congo a month before my 22nd birthday. There, I decided to start my life anew. To me, Rwanda was but a country of horror, nightmares, and bad memories. I vowed I would never go back, hoping to find peace in a foreign land.

However, I later encountered God in a tangible way, and I have discovered that true peace does not depend upon circumstances, nor situations surrounding us, nor where we are. True peace is within and not without. A person could be in jail while their heart is full of joy and peace. This secret to inner joy and peace is obtained through knowing Jesus. Possessing Him is everything in life, now and in the future.

If you are reading this book and you don't have peace, close it for a moment. Accept Christ Jesus as your Lord and Master. Think about Him and see the peace He brings you. Talk to him. Your dialog with Him is called prayer. You may say "Jesus, are you real? If so, reveal yourself to me. Tell me who you truly are! I believe." Jesus is the Prince of Peace. When you call upon Him, He will come, and things will change. There will be peace within you – that's how you know He is real.

Kagame's Propaganda Called Those Who Fled "Genocidaires"

When Rwandans saw Kagame and RPF taking power, the only option remaining for anyone who had insight was to flee the country! How could you stay while you have seen the hostile army taking power? How could you stay when you have seen their atrocities? For many people, there were not many options as to where one can flee. The war pushed us all towards the Western slope towards Gisenyi – it was the only open corridor where RPF had not yet conquered. It was the only passage for many to cross to neighboring countries.

In order to deceive the international community, which had responded to the crisis by the thousands, Kagame told them that all those who fled to Congo were genocidaires or descendants of genocidaires. The expatriates (as we called them) who came from the West to help, oftentimes landed in Kigali where they would be taken through a brief training regarding the region. They would be told that those who would go to Zaire/Congo to help will be going to help genocidaires. Most of the international community believed it.

We did not know how to lobby. We did not know that we had to justify ourselves, and we were so naïve, so innocent, that we were taken advantage and scorned as evil. However, God, who knows the truth from the depth of our heart, gave us great favor. God was with the victims of Kagame and he became our refuge and strength and our real defender.

A refugee in Zaire/DRC. At work with my colleagues at the Lutheran World Federation - Goma 1995

A REFUGEE IN THE CONGO, JULY 1994

O Lord the Most High

You have granted me life

And loving kindness

You blessed me without judging

You loved me without condemning

And Your care has preserved my spirit

It was a hot and dusty summer. There I was, a foreigner on the soil of Congo, then called Zaire. This was Rwanda's neighboring country. I was in the town of Goma following the Rwanda genocide and alone, without my family. I was not home when my family fled the war; alone in Congo I did not know where they were. Each of us had to run to save our own lives. We were all scattered along the way and none of us knew where the others were or whether they were still alive. This was my first time experience out of the country and there I was, homeless and without my family.

Thousands of refugees filled the country of Congo. In this new land, the titles and respect that people had held in Rwanda, or the wealth they had owned, were no longer of value. He who used to own a castle and the one who used to live in a hut were now treated alike. Oh, the riches of this world—not one person could take them from his home to the neighboring country. How much more so, when we pass from life into death? What can one take but life itself? Yet, many people spend all their lives, building their own kingdoms and empires, amassing wealth and riches of their own, and it is all vanity and chasing after the wind!

"I enlarged my works: I built houses for myself, I planted vineyards for myself. I made gardens and parks for myself and I planted in them all kinds of fruit tree. I made ponds of water for myself from which to irrigate a forest of growing trees. I bought male and female slaves and I had homeborn slaves. Also, I possessed flocks and herds larger than all who preceded me in Jerusalem. I collected for myself silver and gold and the treasure of kings and provinces.

I provided for myself male and female singers and the pleasures of men—many concubines. Thus I considered all my activities which my hands had done and the labor which I had exerted, and behold all was vanity and striving after wind." Ecclesiastes 2:4-8; 11

While fleeing and homeless in the streets of Goma, I said to myself, "On what basis will we value the greatness of a man in the after-life world?" My friend Dora, who was with me, commented that it did not matter how great people were—what mattered was how they were going to start their lives anew in that foreign land. I determined that although alone, I would stand strong and do the best I could in life. With the help of God, that dream has been realized today!

Life in a Foreign Land

I settled in Goma as a refugee. My friend Dora and I survived by going around and knocking at doors of rich people, "Hi there! We are Christine and Dora, we are Rwandan refugees. We are educated and can speak at least 5 languages. Would you please give us work to do and let us sleep on your porch?" We knocked at the doors of businesses, residences, and workplaces. For a few nights we slept in the streets, but we quickly left when one day we woke up to find a couple sleeping next to us, and many people were dying of cholera. We continued to knock, and within a week we had found favor with a merchant who let us work for his store, and in exchange we slept inside the store.

Thanks to the education that my family worked hard to give me, and sending me to the language art school, I was able to speak foreign languages. Within the first few weeks, I was employed by International Rescue Committee. I started working as a translator but little by little, I was promoted.

On my first day of work, we were to drive to Kibumba refugee camps to establish new hospitals. I will never forget on that first day, how it took us almost two hours to drive about a dozen miles because of the many dead bodies that filled the sidewalk. These were people who had died fleeing the Rwandan war and genocide. The road was filled with masses of refugees; they looked just like a sea of people. UNHCR estimated that over two million people fled Kagame's arrival into Rwanda. This was the first day for the American International Rescue Committee team, and I don't think they were prepared for what they saw.

On the roadside, a hungry baby was crying next to its dead mother and no other relatives were in sight. Looking past the third roundabout of Goma, we could see thousands of tired refugees crossing the Rwanda/Zaire border. The noise of heavy weapons could be heard in the last battle of the 1994 war. As these refugees fled, walking many miles, the lack of food, water, and shelter caused cholera and other diseases to ravage through them without mercy.

Numerous bodies were lying on the ground under the eucalyptus trees and everywhere you could look. The nearly dead joined the piles of corpses, where they waited for death! These were my compatriots, human beings like me. Seeing them dying like a flower of the field made me wonder about what was happening to them after death.

Few people have seen such horrors! Human language is inadequate to describe the scene of abandoned and lost children crying everywhere; despair was on everyone's face. There was horror and anger, and finally silence. The rescue team was shocked; some of them called it "the road of despair" and others said it was "hell on earth."

That night I could not close my eyes to sleep. Instead, each scene of the horror of this war came into my memory. I had heard of wars. I had learned about World War I and World War II in detail. I had read about them, but in my entire life I never thought I would live through a war. How wrong I was! I lived through this war and the genocide, many times I would find myself in a place where I could hear nothing but the sound of shooting and bombing. I found myself in places where many other people were killed, but not me. Why? Was I a hero?

During those hard times when the war was at its worst, I still had my pocket Bible, which I never read. I would make numerous vows to God: "If only You could protect me now and deliver me through this horrible situation, I would thank You the rest of my life." Oh, the heart of man! How quickly man's heart believes and quickly forgets; quick to make vows and promises but also quick to break them. Quick to say "yes" and act in the "no." As soon I would say my prayers, God would miraculously save my life, but I would forget and move on with life as if I did not make any promises at all. I would take everything for granted and convince myself that I was somehow a hero.

In Congo, thousands of refugees lived in camps. I lived in the city of Goma where I had a good job, having been hired first by the International Rescue Committee. Then, after they left, I was promoted to work with another NGO that paid better, and had more benefits.

In 1994, while employed at the International Rescue Committee in Goma, I met someone special whom God has used to fulfill many of my dreams, Gregg Grunenfelder. Gregg became my boss while I was employed at the International Rescue Committee and we quickly became good friends. Gregg did not stay too long in Goma. After three months he returned to the United States, but we kept in touch. He and his wife, Catherine, gave to me generously. Three years later they would bring me to the United States, support me, and pay for all of my schooling fees.

In Goma, I met many wonderful people who came from all over the world to help refugees. May God grant them all His blessings and remember them all in time of need.

"The Lord protects the strangers; He supports the fatherless and the widow." Psalm 145:9

While in Goma working for the International Rescue Committee helping refugees, I found out that some members of my family had survived the war and were in Bukavu, another town in Zaire. My younger sister, Chantal had survived the war. I brought her to live with me and, thank God, we both migrated to the U.S.

9

RWANDA COMMITTING ATROCITIES, KILLINGS / GENOCIDE IN THE CONGO

CAUGHT UP IN ANOTHER WAR: THE CONGO WAR

I have never seen the evil reigning in Rwanda anywhere else. I have heard of wars. I have heard of refugees, but I have never heard of a government that crosses over the border of a neighboring sovereign nation to raid, to ambush, and to kill those who fled the government. I have never seen where a government pursues refugees to bring them back by force.

Two years after the 1994 genocide, Kagame started another war in the Congo/Zaire where, according to the U.N.'s Mapping Report[1], some of the worst crimes in the history of the world took place, the killing of millions of innocent Congolese and Rwandans. There they killed the weak, the sick, children, women, and people who posed no threat.

The two million Rwanda refugees settled in neighboring countries, but mostly in Congo/ Zaire. It was said that Kagame would not have peace knowing that the very same people he tried so hard to kill and destroy were just a few miles across the border of Rwanda and the Congo. So, Kagame attacked Congo to force refugees back into Rwanda, but also to loot Congo. By the end of 1996, the army of Rwanda had attacked Congo and the cities of Goma and Bukavu were under heavy fighting.

In June 1996, I remember sitting for the last time in my beautiful office in Goma while all the Westerners were planning to evacuate, leaving us behind. They loved me but they could not take me. I could not get a Visa. It was a terrible, dark day. The war became so bad – shootings and bombings were everywhere around us. There was no escape and no one to call. Besides, the phones had gone dead because of the war. From the office I had to run home and make my way through fierce shootings. How hard it was, to go through a war again, and in a foreign country.

Like the Rwandan war, when this Goma war started, our lives were in danger. Those who were believed to be on Rwanda's side (whether true or supposed) were arrested. Chantal, my sister, had been arrested by the Congo army because they said she was a Rwandan Tutsi. I heard it from work, and I rushed to pay a ransom. We negotiated, and I gave them a couple of hundred dollars so they did not keep her too long. I rushed to those I believed were my true friends, to see if they could hide her for me. To my surprise, one by one they refused to hide her even for one night. I cried, "Listen, that's all I have left! Her life is in danger; they want to kill her!" But no one cared. None was moved, and no one was willing to in fear they would be killed or arrested if my sister were found in their homes.

I rushed back to the new apartment I had rented. The landlord lived in the same complex, and he wanted us out. He said he did not want my sister to stay with us, for she was certain to bring trouble. He told me, "It is better for her to die alone rather than all of us." How incredibly selfish! He added that if I insisted that she stay, he would make sure all of us were out of there as well. But how could I let my sister wander around without shelter while I was given one? I looked up and sought help from above. Immediately a friend I never thought would help showed up and offered to take her to her home for a while.

Evening came so quickly. As the battle between the armies of Congo and Rwanda became intense, many people left their homes to run away to the mountains. Goma became desolate, and so were the camps of refugees where many thousands had lived in shelter. The landlord urged us also to leave; he was changing his mind by the minute. He said he did not want to be in trouble for having Rwandans at his property.

I looked outside and saw that a storm was raging. It was raining, and thunder and lightning were everywhere. I'd experienced many flights from dangerous situations, but I wondered if I would ever make it out of this one! I was about to obey the landlord and run to the mountains, but the landlord did not want to give the deposit for three month's rent. So, we finally stayed because he did not want to lose that money. Many people and friends who ran to the mountains never made it back. Many died because they were shot during the war; others died of disease.

While everyone at the landlord's complex was hiding under their beds and in the basement because of the shootings, I was forced by the landlord to climb up and stay in the attic where we could hardly breathe, and were exposed. We stayed there all night long. Intense shooting and bombings were taking place nearby where we lived. I watched in the night and saw the biggest house near us hit by Katyusha. It was destroyed.

During that night, I could not close my eyes. Instead, my spirit started wandering. Over a period of two long years I had run from the Rwandan war. And here I was again, under the same war and worst of all, I was in a foreign country. Through the noise of heavy weapons, I remembered God. I had heard about God before; I even went to church every Sunday, I even used to call upon when I was in trouble, but I did not have a real relationship with him. Right there, in between life and death, I realized that I was lost without Him. Very soon, there would be no food or water!

"God, please save my life. If you save me from this war, I will serve you the rest of my life. I will tell people of what you have done for me. I will tell them that you save and deliver." That night I sincerely prayed, but I did not know what serving God meant! Dare to talk to God because, my friend, He answers prayers. He answered me and I made it through the night and the days to follow. It is about this time that I sincerely committed my life to Jesus. I have written about my conversion in my other book, "The Blazing Holy Fire."[2] You can read that book to know about my conversion and the story of growing up in Rwanda.

After this, we spent about four days without communicating with my sister Chantal, nor did we venture out of the apartment complex. My prayers were that she would not run to the mountains where many died fleeing the war. God is faithful, and a few days later we were reunited. The war was not yet over but subsided. We survived this awful war by the power of God, but millions of lives were lost during Rwanda invasion into the Congo. May God remember our prayers and bring peace in The Great Lakes Region.

After re-uniting with my sister, we returned to Rwanda. Though the wars and genocide were over in Rwanda, security remained an issue. Three years after the genocide, inside Rwanda, many people went to sleep not knowing if they would wake up alive. In the remote areas, far from the main road, far from the sight of people, Rwanda soldiers killed, kidnapped, and destroyed left and right. They did not do it without the knowledge of the government. Proof is that there was no investigation. During this time, you could not even take your case to the police. Especially Hutus, they had no say in their own country.

THE KILLINGS OF CIVILIANS IN KALIMA, DRC CONGO

My two brothers, Regis and Pascal, were also refugees in Bukavu. When Rwanda attacked Congo, my dear two brothers were killed by the Rwandan army when they were found to be educated Hutus. This happened in the fall of 1996.

My sister-in-law, Rose, was there and she survived these killings to bring us the story. It was explained to us by Rose, that on the night when my two brothers were killed, they were together with other refugees fleeing the Congo war. A group of armed RPF soldiers came and separated men from women. This tactic would often be used by those who killed and when they made a separation, my sister-in-law could not help crying, knowing it was her last time to see her husband.

They were ordered by these soldiers to give them any belongings they had. After confiscating their belongings, the army shot all the males to death, one-by-one, starting with those in whose bag a degree of any kind was found. Regis and Pascal were educated. Regis was an architect teacher and Pascal was a professional soccer player and also worked at the mayor's office. They were the first to be killed. My sister-in-law managed to make her way back to Rwanda in the fall of 1996, and reported to us of their killings.

My heart was broken that they were shot because they were educated Hutus. This is not something they chose. God did not ask them before they were born whether they wanted to be Tutsis or Hutus. My brothers, who even saved Tutsis during the genocide, were killed. After the genocide, some Tutsis whom they saved came looking for my brothers to say thank you for hiding them but they could not find them.

The Rwandan soldiers whom we met in Goma and befriended us said they had received orders from above that said, "In Goma, since there is a strong International presence, do not kill." Indeed, when the Goma war subsided in the summer of 1996, journalists and all kinds of humanitarian workers were present. So, during that time, Rwanda soldiers behaved like holy boys and did not kill in the presence of westerners. However, they killed in secrecy. In Bukavu where the war happened at the same time, the westerners' presence was very limited, and there they were told to kill refugees. And killing, they did even in the view of others.

Forgiveness

I pity those who kill, because they do not know what they are doing. He who kills others once, kills himself twice. He who kills is a loser and not a winner. Killing might give people a temporary win, but it is a deceiving victory which, in turn, kills the killer. Hell fire is reserved for murderers. It is my prayer that murderers who are still alive repent, ask for forgiveness, learn to forgive themselves, and, once for all, shun evil.

God helped me to forgive the killers. I forgave and I forgot and I have moved on. I am not angry at them because the moment I gave my life to Jesus, He healed me of all the bitterness and wounds from the past. God filled my heart with His love. My heart breaks for the millions of people who died, and are still dying, inside Rwanda. This is one of the reasons why I have written this book—to be their voice.

Forgiveness is a must to be free. Forgiveness is a must to move forward.

My brother Francois Regis Dirimasi was killed by the RPF in Kalima / Zaire DRC in 1996 together with his younger brother

THE KILLINGS OF RWANDA CLERGY IN KALIMA, DRC CONGO[3]

These were Rwandan priests, nuns, and some brothers in exile. On February 25, 1997, they were surrounded by Rwanda army in Congo. They knew the worst was coming. They took this picture before they died. There are friends who have survived this Kalima massacre, I pray they make their story known one day. May God remember their bloodshed!

This photo was taken in front of the Kalima church in the DRC a few minutes before their assassination On February 25, 1997. [3]

The Church of Rwanda Victims - Their Martyrdom in Kalima in DRC(ex-Zaïre).[2]

The Rwandan clergy had left the Bukavu region to flee the massacres of refugees and the fighting between the troops of the former dictator and President of Zaire, Mobutu Sese Seko Kuku Ngbendu Wa Za Banga, and the rebels of Kabila who were supported by the Rwandan Army. Then they were assassinated.

The priest victims are the Abbots: Antoine Hategekimana, Emmanuel Munyakazi, Jean Uwizeyimana, Norbert Milimo,

François-Xavier Muyoboke, Urbain Twagirayezu, Etienne Kabera, and Augustin Nkulikiyumukiza. The sisters are Marie-Francine Nyirarukundo and Félicité Mukamihigo, belonging to the Congregation of the Sisters -François d'Assise, whose mother house is in Brakel in Belgium, as well as sister Clotilde Nyirabakungu, belonging to the Rwandan Congregation of Abizeramariya.

The Assassination of Mgr. Muzihirwa Mwenengabo, the Archbishop of Bukavu[4]

The number of clergy killed in Kalima does not include the clergy killed elsewhere in the Congo such as the killing of Mgr. Muzihirwa Mwenengabo, the Archbishop of Bukavu.

Mgr. Mwenengabo had condemned the invasion of Rwandan soldiers into Congo. He was an activist, a vocal supporter of human rights. On October 28, 1996, the Rwandan troops poured into the eastern part of Zaire and he issued a final and fervent plea for aid and for peace, and in his radio message said, "We hope that God will not abandon us and that from some part of the world will rise for us a small flare of hope."[4]

In the afternoon of October 29, 1996, Rwandan soldiers attacked his convoy. They got hold of him, proceeded to interrogate him through torture before shooting him on the spot.

As you can see, so many clergy members were killed by the

RPF. Even to this day, any clergy member who does not pledge their allegiance to Kagame and his RPF are seen as enemies and they are also targeted.

The world instead of condemning such atrocities and bringing to justice those who committed such acts, they fell into deception of Kagame, who would justify every killing. They began to praise Kagame of his economic miracles. Others turned the other way and would not condemn such barbaric acts. By doing so, they encouraged a culture of impunity. By doing so, they emboldened Kagame. The time has come for justice to be done. I am asking the international community to investigate and participate in leading justice to victory.

10

POST GENOCIDE IN RWANDA – NOW: RULING WITH IRON FIST

A POLITIC OF REVENGE AND ELIMINATION

After the Rwanda genocide, justice was applied to those Hutus who killed. The International Criminal Tribunal for Rwanda (ICTR) was established to judge them and also in Rwanda the traditional Gacaca court was used to handle thousands of cases. However, real just has never been applied to Kagame and his RPF. Therefore, after winning the Rwanda war, some of the murderers who shed much blood became judges, lawyers, the witnesses, and the jury. The Rwanda justice system was hijacked and truth was chased from the land.

Kagame came full of wrath and of revenge! From Uganda where he served as Museveni's head of the Military Intelligence of Uganda, everyone knew him. He was nicknamed Pilato (from Pontius Pilate of the Bible) – the brutal torturer and killer. Upon arriving in Rwanda, he showed that he wasn't just above the law, he was the law. He institutionalized ethnic discrimination and he held dearly to the status quo of Tutsi-domination and the main characteristic of the ruling Tutsi bourgeoise was to promote Tutsi supremacy. To this day, no Hutu or Twa is allowed in Kagame's presidential guard or special forces.

He came to crush Hutus who were the majority. He killed many and put many others in jail – especially those with PhD's, master's degrees, lawyers, doctors, public servants, the wisest of the wise, and the most noble man, as long as they were Hutus. He came with an agenda to eliminate them and, if not possible, to cripple them and crush them until they are never able to lead again.

I have shared with you the unclassified document from the state department that showed how after the genocide, about 10,000 people were being killed every month. There are other journalists who have written similar accounts. Their reports are out there on the internet.

Men of Noble Character Imprisoned

My brother Jean Damascene was such a man of noble character. He held an engineering degree from a European university and was once CEO of the first company that produced cooking oil in Rwanda. During the time of war however, he was heavily persecuted because of his Tutsi wife. When Kagame took power, Jean Damascene, who at first had taken refuge in Kibeho, was then thrown in jail in 1994, while before God and before men, he had done nothing wrong. My brother was a peacemaker, an intelligent great man. No matter how we advocated, no matter how we knocked, they kept him locked up in jail for 13 years.

He was thrown in jail immediately after the genocide. It was reported to us that people whom he doesn't know, nor had ever seen in his life, accused him of participating in the Rwanda genocide. During that time, people were filled with revenge and all it took to qualify to be thrown in jail, or to be killed, was to be an educated, wealthy male coming from especially Hutu tribe. Tutsis who were seen as critics or who did not want to contribute to the RPF were not spared either. Besides revenge, RPF hired professional false witnesses whose job was to accuse and testify against innocent people. During this time, being a Hutu was like a big crime.

These people who came against my brother Jean had confiscated his house and a commercial building that he owned. For years, they occupied them. After much prayer and fasting, pleading and begging, my brother was cleared by Gacaca court when it was obvious that his accusers were people who did not even know who he was and their testimonies kept contracting each other. Finally, by God's grace, my brother was released, but oftentimes the people who lived in his property sought to kill him. He had to flee the country.

During all these years of imprisonment, my brother, like other prisoners, was not allowed to be visited except two or three minutes per week. I remember while I was still in Rwanda, before coming to the U.S., I used to visit him on Saturdays. We would bring him food every day and there were long lines, hundreds of people waiting to see their loved ones. At the sound of the whistle, we would run to meet the prisoner who came and stood by a long horizontal line. We would quickly greet, pass on a quick message and hand him the food and run back as soon as possible. If one delayed, they would be beaten by the police. Some Saturdays were special days, when they would grant about 2 to 3 minutes to talk.

There, in the country they boast so much about, I saw how animals had better rights than any prisoner there.

Jean Damascene was a man who loved and was loved by many. He is the man who sought the welfare of all Rwandans but look what he was rewarded instead. God had blessed him, and there are many people who have an education thanks to him. So, upon arriving in Rwanda, Kagame's RPF put him in jail, seized all his estates and they took away his privilege to raise his four boys.

Even at the publishing of this book, Rwanda prisons are filled with great wonderful people, like you dearest reader. Great, great people who have never committed a crime – the only crime they have committed is being a human rights defender, or to be born Hutus or Christian or Tutsis who dares to speak their minds and criticize the government of injustice. These prisons have been filling up since 1994. The prisons fill up so much that at times, they have to kill people to make more room for new prisoners.

RPF soldiers put some people in containers right after they took the country and locked them for days, in the midst of a hot summer, until they were all dead. Such was the case of Michelle Runyinya's mother . Runyinya went to the same Lycée that I attended. Her mother was killed this way. There were many people thrown in cisterns or large holes or swamps, and they died this way.

Kibeho massacres[1] [2]

Kibeho was one of the zones controlled by the French as part of Opération Turquoise within Rwanda. Many Hutus who did not flee into the neighboring countries took refuge at Kibeho camp. When the French troops withdrew after the victory of the RPF in August 1994, Kibeho camp was taken over by the UNAMIR and a number of NGO's. On April 22, 1995, without much notice, Kagame's army took over the camp and began to destroy it, killing refugees without mercy.

Australian troops witnessed the massacre. It is believed that about 4,000 to 8,000 Rwandan Hutu people, maybe more were mercilessly massacred by the RPA (the military wing of the RPF) at the Kibeho Camp for Internally Displaced Persons in

Southwestern Rwanda. The Rwanda regime said that only 338 people lost their lives. No one has ever been prosecuted for these crimes. Kylie Stevenson has written a good article about this[3] you can read it at https://www.ntnews.com.au/news/northern-territory/australian-troops-remember-kibeho-massacre-in-rwanda/news-story/1c6be840029a30cb1be26b0f3b96242c

Also there are books that have been written about this massacre including: *Pure Massacre* by Kevin O'Halloran; *Combat Medic* by Terry Pickard, and *The Easy Day was Yesterday* by Paul Jordan.

THE RPF BINDING VOW THAT HAS CURSED MANY

RPF came, taking over and forcing people to become their members. Every member of RPF must make a vow. Rwandans who have not vowed within the RPF cannot be trusted. Great honor and favors are given to those individuals who vow. The vow[4] is binding, and it is one of the worst curses ever, since it is made to a government body. I have translated the vow which can be found many places on internet and social medias. This vow has been said by so many in Rwanda and it became a great snare for them.

"If I forsake the vow, let me be crucified like the enemy."

Moving forward and never shrinking back,

I ....

I vow before the following members of RPF, confirming that I understand well the RPF/Inkotanyi consitution which is dedicated to the development of all Rwandans, whether young, or old or even the future generation for them to have proper value in our nation and even in other nations wherever they might be.

I vow, agreeing and promising, that I will unite with every member of RPF/Inkotanyi now and in the future. I agree that I must understand that everyone in the RPF/Inkotanyi must protect, be protected, be advised, and submit to the given counsel so that we protect ourselves from all the evil that befell our nation and on those who live in it.

I also agree that I will join hands with others to fight against Rwanda's enemies, wherever they may be.

In the eyes and presence of these members, I vow that I will follow all the laws and commands of RPF/Inkotanyi, the ones which are, and which will be. I will avoid making mistakes, I will not betray, nor procrastinate nor make other mistakes that have caused our nation to plunge into the darkness.

Dear members who are here, if I ever betray this declaration, If I ever do what is contrary to this constitution and the laws and commands governing RPF/Inkotanyi,

It means that I have betrayed each Rwandan, and if I do so, may I be crucified like an enemy.

Post-Genocide Revival

Standing in the midst of death, going through the valley of death, many people cried out to God. Even when one does not believe in God, in the face of death, one of the very few options left for the people is to cry out to God. In crying out to Him, people came to find God. Revival broke out throughout Rwanda. In the midst of suffering and various adversity, many Tutsis in exile found God and they brought Him to Rwanda. Tutsis are great wonderful people. Kagame has tarnished their names. After the genocide, many people poured out their sorrows and pains to God and as a result, a great number of Rwanda citizens became born again Christians.

In 1997, I witnessed a revival that was real and vibrant in Rwanda. During lunch hour, most offices in downtown Kigali would close and the saints would meet at Inkuru Nziza for two hours of great worship, the word, and great fellowship. The service was every day and great miracles, signs, and wonders took place in our midst.

At the time, Kagame was Vice President and at the same time the Minister of Defense but truly, he was the shadow government. He was the one who ran everything, and he had the last say in every matter, in every branch of the government. He acted like he was above the law and everybody feared him. He was the only one with the last say over the executive, judiciary, and legislative branch – a true dictator.

Kagame must have heard of the revival taking place at this place, and very soon, his Directorate of Military Intelligence DMI started flocking into church services. Government informants of all sorts began flocking into these meetings and began to report on Hutu pastors who were part of the fellowship.

Hutu pastors began to be persecuted. A great wave of imprisonments hit them, but some Tutsi pastors from this fellowship became bold and rebuked the government for its wicked behavior. Nonetheless, Hutu pastors were still imprisoned. Kagame, being a heathen himself, held great grudges against Christians because he said Tutsis died inside the church. Upon his return to Rwanda, the blameless clergy members that we all respected, were thrown in jail and killed. In the meantime, his lobbyists were lobbying for him in the West and in the Vatican that these were genocidaires. As I have shared before, his grudges against Christianity has its origin way before the genocide and dates back to the colonial period.

11

RPF'S PLANS TO DESTROY EXILES ABROAD

———

The Ministry Injustice and The Department of Lies

After RPF took power, with some of the perpetrators becoming new judges, many innocent Hutus became the guilty ones. Even some of the Tutsis who had nice homes and lands were thrown in jail so that the newcomers could possess their estates. The oppressed were labeled the oppressor. Some of the murderers took power to govern and to investigate.

Kagame ruled with a fist of iron, and injustice became one of his best friends. His regime denied justice to the Hutus and jailed them without mercy. The Ministry of Justice became the Ministry of Injustice, where they would fabricate cases of innocent people they jailed. A new thing began in Rwanda, where they would teach people how to falsely accuse, and how to falsely testify. Many times, they hired witnesses who had never met the accused person.

One of their big departments, to this day, is the department of deception. They spend money, effort, and energy inventing lies. Those who grew up in Rwanda had never seen such things.

Weaponizing Genocide

They began to use genocide as a weapon. If someone spoke up, they labeled them as genocidaires. If anyone criticized what they did, they threatened them and accused them with genocide ideology. When politicians rose up to form a party or run against the president, they accused them of being genocide deniers and threw them in jail.

The former president and anyone who tried to challenge Kagame in the presidential race were thrown in jail. Genocide became a weapon to destroy anyone who dared to speak up. Genocide was also used to gain sympathy and aid from foreign governments. It became a means for gain.

LEAKED PHONE CONVERSATION BETWEEN TWO OF KAGAME'S TOP OFFICIALS, AND THEIR PLANS TO DESTROY DISSIDENTS ABROAD

The information here is a leaked conversation, coming straight from Kagame's two top officials who are part of intelligence and death squads. I translated this audio from Kinyarwanda to English. It is top secret. They are planning character assassinations of dissidents, and how to kill dissidents abroad.

Come and take a look inside Kagame's spies and death squads. Hear how they work, how they threaten those who refuse their suicidal missions. They talk about how they eliminate innocent people and how they poison them. They are making plans to kill Paul Rusesabagina, the producer of Hotel Rwanda who saved over a thousand people during the genocide. Learn how they fabricate cases against innocent people and drag them to court using their powerful lawyers abroad. Hear this and take it to your justice department, all the way to Attorney General William Barr, and warn them of such plots.

Hear how they manipulate people. They are boasting also on how they have poisoned their critics abroad, and people thought it was cancer. They lament how their missions have been failing lately, and this has caused Kagame to put pressure on them.

"He does not give us a moment to sleep," they say. There is a network of spies abroad; they are sent as a team, but this team has another team that spies on them and monitors them, to make sure they are doing the right thing. They are planning to use, if necessary, cyber-attacks to hack into computers of dissidents, to install child pornography and fabricate crimes against them to the FBI and the American Justice Department. One of their big targets in this conversation is Paul Rusesabagina who also gave me this leaked conversation.

Who Is Paul Rusesabagina?[1][2]

Paul Rusesabagina is a Rwandan humanitarian, known as the "African brave-hearted hotel manager" who, during the 1994 Rwanda genocide, saved 1,268 Hutus and Tutsis, hiding them in the Belgian four-star hotel he managed. His courageous acts inspired the Academy Award-nominated film Hotel Rwanda (2004), in which he was portrayed by American actor Don Cheadle. During the Rwandan genocide, none of those refugees were hurt or killed during the attacks. Rusesabagina is a recipient of the Presidential Medal of Freedom from President George W. Bush, and has received many awards.

Though Paul Rusesabagina saved many Tutsis and Hutus in the hotel he managed (it was the only place that I know of where genocide did not take place), Paul Kagame sought to harm him. Rusesabagina once told me how an RPF soldier was sent with a pistol to kill him at his house in Kigali but by God's grace, he and his family escaped to Belgium. Since then, Kagame has incited many in Rwanda and in the west to have mixed feelings about him. It is a problem in when a leader incites his subjects to hate citizens. May God who sees, help to weed out the poisonous root of bitterness in the midst of this beautiful country.

How This Document Was Leaked to Us

In 2019, an anonymous person called Paul Rusesabagina's

family and said, "You have saved my life during the genocide. God forbid that I will betray innocent blood." He then sent the audio to the family over the phone and disappeared. Rusesabagina's family tried to reach back to him in vain. Even the number he used to send was no longer in service. It was a warning and one that is real. The two men talking over the phone are known top officials in Kagame's intelligence circle. This is an authentic conversation and in the hands of law enforcement. Rusesabagina has the original audio and it was broadcasted on Radio Ubumwe YouTube Channel[3]. A copy is also on www.christinecoleman.org. From the time it was sent to Rusesabagina, it spread through the internet and social media. The conversation makes me think of a meeting in hell between demons.

The Leaked Conversation

MR A: Yes, sir.

MR B: How are you?

MR A: We are ok, sir.

MR B: What is going on? Your reports don't look good anymore. Is there any problem? What's
lacking in your unit?

MR A: Yeah, I see… Sir, we've been busy these days. It's not easy, but we are trying our best. I think everything is being put together, then you'll receive all the reports, sir.

MR B: Too busy to go and meet Eugenie, and ask her about the plan to testify against Cyumbati? What do you mean being busy?

MR A: Well, we managed to meet that lady ...we met her and talked, but she keeps on acting as a stupid Christian, saying that she can't falsely testify against anyone!

MR B: But does Christianity exist in this, does Christianity exist in our suicide missions?

MR A: Leave her alone for now, we got her...I think we can use her in our other missions because we fully have her on our side everywhere, she can't escape.

MR B: Ok...You know, I was wondering why you never gave me any feedback about her, but that is not today's big concern! Today I just called you to ask about the deal of Andrea and Cyumbati. How can we proceed with that deal? Our boss (Muzehe i.e. Kagame) is putting pressure on us...he doesn't give us even a moment to sleep.

MR A: Oh ok, I see! I think ....we should get someone else to use in the deal of Andrea and Antoinette...Hmmm... Eeh... to make things easier we can get someone who can easily reach out to them...I am afraid that using that lady is a risk because she may go and disappear. Then our mission can fail...it may be like the other mission we failed lately...that's why we need to avoid any mistake in planning against Andrea and Antoinette.

MR B: You need to be very careful, because these days a lot of operations are failing and our boss [Kagame] is not happy with that. How about using Gisimba? Do you think it would accomplish something?

MR A: Ohhhh ok. Yes, great idea, we can use Gisimba, but how can we use him?

MR B: We have some devices which have videos and pictures with child pornography. We can give them to Gisimba so that he can try to spread them around…I don't know if you have ever seen those devices…Just stop by the office so that we can show them to you.

MR A: What do you mean, sir?

MR B: Devices that that we have at the office that contain child pornography….we can give those devices to Gisimba so that he can make sure that they are installed on the computers of those whom we seek to bring down.

MR A: Yeah, yeah, yeah! I know those…hmmmmm… yeah…that may work…

MR B: Yes

MR A: We can give them to him.

MR B: Yes

MR A: Then after giving them to him….ahhhh

MR B: If we give those to him, then he manages to install

them there, we can figure out how we can use our guys in RIB who, in turn, can report it to FBI. Then FBI would do a search and find out that their computers have those pornographies... We can make it in a top secret way as we usually do in such operations ...It is a big crime in those countries if someone is caught with child pornography.

MR A: Yes, that sounds like a great plan, but is there any way we can publish it first in our propaganda news?

MR B: Yeah...we must print that in Rushyashya [Rushyashya is Kagame's propaganda newspaper, which he uses for character assassination of his opponents. It is a newspaper that spews out lies and deceit.] Rushyashya should publish an article that explains it well, showing even those pictures...but you need to make sure you first proofread them well before our guys who work for us in Rushyashya publish it ...because, you know, there are some articles which we have carelessly published before, then we were obliged to delete them just because of carelessness. I hope that you remember how some army commanders came here to explain themselves further.

MR A: Oh, yes, you know well that it may work, but those people have a big network such as Rusesabagina and the Doctor....ahhhh, I didn't know...Do you think that it can be easy for Gisimba to reach out to Doctor and to Rusesabagina?

MR B: Not really hard...Once the article is published by

Rushyashya, then we can use our application means to share them in their computers…It would not be that difficult.

MR A: Oh, ok.

MR B: You know that our spies abroad who are computer savvy are not sleeping…They are working, and we have no problem on the technical side of it.

MR A: Yes, yes, I see…So, we can use our app then?

MR B: Yes, the usual app that we normally use.

MR A: So, we can get them installed on Rusesabagina and Doctor's computers without anyone knowing a thing of it.

MR B: Oh, yes…Never commit any foolish mistakes again – you remember what happened last month.

MR A: I remember…That guy really betrayed us, but…

MR B: Make sure to review them before they are published in Rushyashya, as you know those pictures our guy who lives in Belgium took for us, where Andrea and Karemye were committing adultery in Belgium.

MR A: Yes.

MR B: That means you are not allowed to let anything get published before they bring them into your office for review and approval…We are facing a lot of issues.

MR A: I see. So, we can figure out how to combine it with the tourists news…

MR B: Oh, yes, this will help us a lot as our lawyers will

check and find rumors that Antoinette spread to Americans, then they will despise all the rumors. Antoinette will lose credibility... So, we need to carefully plan everything.

MR A: Yes, we must do everything, and make sure that Antoinette loses credibility, like exposing her on how she abandoned her mother during the war, how she left her while she had means to evacuate her, and how she left behind her brothers and father while they were killing people.

MR B: Yes.

MR A: You know they were highly ranked Interahamwe (killers).

MR B: Yes.

MR A: I think we can even link this to the latest family party they organized for their mother. I saw the pictures. Then we can make sure it is known as if they wanted to apologize to her in her last stage of her life, and make it look like they wanted her forgiveness before her death.

MR B: No time to waste in this dossier. You must make sure that everything works smoothly.

MR A: Sir? If ...

MR B: Make sure you follow all guidelines, make sure that everything is well lined up.

MR A: Yes, yes, sir. But what if Gisimba refuses to help? What can we do if he refuses this mission?

MR B: He can't make that mistake. Remember, you still have his recordings with his prostitutes from here.

MR A: Oh, yeah.

MR B: And he should be reminded that he cannot survive if he is given the Munyuza water. [Poison that Rwanda death squads give that causes cancer.] But he normally does not resist us. I think Gisimba is not an issue.

MR A: Yeah, he will not give us trouble because we have those recordings with his Kigali prostitutes. We need to use them to threaten him, even make it public a little bit, and make him understand that it would be a serious problem if his wife learns about his infidelity…and I think…

MR B: Don't bother yourself that much because we have another team that monitors all the steps those people make, and in case our trick does not work, the team manages to get closer to them, and then we can kill them as we normally do. So, don't be concerned that much because Afande (i.e. The Boss, Kagame) has empowered them strongly and appointed another powerful team to monitor them.

MR A: But I think there is another element that we may need to help us.

MR B: Ok.

MR A: You see that woman, Mukandagano.

MR B: I know her…

MR A: I think she is one of ours, and we can use her.

MR B: Yeah, we have her.

MR A: Yeah, we own her because if we manage to prove that she is behind her white husband's death…the one that we just killed by making him drink the Munyuza water (poison).

MR B: Oh that one! People thought that he died of cancer.

MR A: Yeah, you see if we manage to prove that we killed him.

MR B: You know that's easy.

MR A: She can know that things are not that simple. She can realize that she can't play games with us.

MR B: Yes.

MR A: And she can agree to do everything we command her to do.

MR B: No jokes. If this doesn't work… in case it doesn't work, we will try other means and we have no problem doing that.

MR A: After Antoinette loses credibility then, there is nothing else she can say that would be valued. You know she is the one who was interpreting for those white tourists regarding all those cases.

MR B: Yes.

MR A: As for Antoinette's sister who lives in Belgium, apart from the liaison she has with that priest, we need to prove how she travels to France to fornicate with that man who happened to be her fiancé….ehhh, who is that man again?

MR B: Do you mean Venuste?

MR A: Yeah. That's it, Venuste. That same Venuste.

MR B: Yes, that also should be linked in to make it sound more powerful.

MR A: Yes.

MR B: Do you know that you just reminded me about the affair, that Gisimba once told us how they tricked that white man by telling him lies – that the taxmen raped Antoinette while they were in Kenya, then they got a lot of money from the white guy. You know those people are also serial thieves. In all we need to accomplish this mission because…

MR A: You see, Antoinette sister told lies to the white guy, that the taxman raped her…because she just wanted to get money.

MR B: You know, it was to give the money to the priest, our informants ended up telling us that.

MR A: Then in this way… you even see the dossier of RLM, of Paul Rusesabagina, by then we would have destroyed their characters, they will be feeling pressure from Americans, it is then we would publish the dossier of Mugimba. You should remember then that.

MR B: Rusesabagina in Europe…?

MR A: Reaching him is not that easy, but there are many ways we may use. Rugira and his team, they could make him drink the Munyuza water (poison that kills one like cancer) but getting to Rusesabagina is not that easy. We have put teams after him, up to three teams to no avail, but you know it will work?

MR A: You see the Rugimba dossier. You know that Antoinette is the one who brought him from Dakar to Europe. So, we can fabricate a case of trafficking of people.

MR B: But we already fabricated that trafficking case against him…

MR A: Frank, you remember Rugogwe… you know that he really disappointed us, but you know he got his own share. That's why in this case we must be extremely careful so that not a single mistake is made.

MR A: Just yesterday, they were rebuking me, saying that we are accomplishing nothing. That they are giving us all the money there is, the funds, we have the young men that we are not using.

MR B: There are problems, problems everywhere.

MR A: But you know, this Antoinette has given us a headache for a very long time, do you remember that? That's why we must do a follow up closely. Do you remember that she is the one who worked with the French of Zone Turquoise? She would be informing the Sendashonga? The Nkubito? They might have been working together with her.

MR B: There is one report I was reading…it is a lot of things here. So, how can we plan this? I was told that in two weeks at least, we must show them something. If there is something that is not working, if it is for the lack of information… that we … how would you go about this?

MR A: I understand that… now as for … do you remember the case of Lizinde?

MR B: I know she is behind those who shot him, behind those young men, even she lost one of her relatives right there. Bugirimfura. Do you remember that?

MR A: Yeah! You see even Bugirimfura relatives do not know that she was behind it, so…

MR B: There might be some of them who learned about it and went to the police to inquire… True, the police called me, and I told them that this is not a police issue.

MR A: You see if her relatives learn about this, Mukandagano would be fearful and know that she must help us so that we may finish it well. Anyways, have you been in South Africa lately?

MR B: Yes, I have been in those cities, I met with the wife of Java and we talked.

MR A: Is Java here? In Rwanda?

MR B: Yeah, he is, but even with his wife can help … I

talked to his wife, there won't be an issue in South Africa. All things are lined up in South Africa.

MR A: Have you found him to be a person who can help us?

MR B: Don't worry about South Africa. South Africa is easy, the hard ones are the ones in America, and only a little bit. How can someone from South Africa resist us? You know I even talked to his wife, and there was no problem. Even in two days, I will meet with Java before he goes back. I do not know his plan when he is going back.

MR A: Ok, thanks. Then tomorrow we meet at the safe house. [A place where Rwanda incarcerate people, torture them and detain them unlawfully.]

MR B: Let's meet at the safe house where we usually meet. There is someone that I am to interview there. You know there are so many people we imprison there and when you delay getting there, you find out that they have been killed already. There are so many people, so many people that we are running out of space where to imprison them. There is new information of someone we caught from South Africa I will be coming to look for... Let's meet at 10 o'clock, so that I can give you those devices and you will find a way to get them to Gisimba.

MR A: Thank you

MR B: Alright, and when I will give them to you, I will give some updates and some briefings and other things to annex to it.

MR A: Ok, thanks a lot.

The end of the conversation…

These are Rwanda top officers plotting evil to carry out terrorist acts inside and outside the country. Assassinating, poisoning, killing and destroying their critics. These are the people who have led Rwanda for the past 26 years. These are leaders who work unrighteousness; these are people who plot injustice. These are leaders who build a city with bloodshed; who establishes a town by iniquity.

I am asking the U.S. Department and the Department of Justice to investigate these things and to impose sanctions against Kagame and his top assassins.

I am asking the U.S. Department of Justice to read this book and hear the true stories of those who have been victims of Rwanda Injustice and to review cases of those USA citizens whom the government of Rwanda has accused of committing genocide in the past, now, and in the future.

TERRORISTS IN OUR MIDST

Not too long ago, a Rwandan intelligence man was boasting on social media how Rwanda intelligence is all over the world. It is true that they have their network of spies all over. The money that was supposed to develop the country is thrown in a trash like this. These spies work through Rwanda embassies and Rwanda Diasporas which are created and logistically financed by Rwanda's intelligence. The head of Rwanda Diaspora abroad is usually the point of contact for the intelligence. All over the world, wherever there is a good number of Rwandans, respective Rwandan embassies help them to create local committees called Rwanda Diaspora.

Rwanda who came fleeing the regime usually do not go to those diaspora but in recent years, Rwanda has been aggressively recruiting refugees who fled the regime through deception. Rwandan agents come to them acting like they are bringing peace, love and unity. In some cases, they buy them out by offering them free flight tickets and a free stay in a five-star hotel in Rwanda. Sometimes, they promise to give them great positions in the Rwandan government. There are many who fell into these traps. They were lucky to leave Rwanda alive, they become successful in exile but when they fall to the deception and go back, sometimes they disappear and there are some who are languishing in

Kagame's prisons today.

Kagame has his spies and death squads operating across Africa, even in the west to silence critics and even if possible, to eliminate them. They are opportunists who are attracted by money. I heard one who was boasting how the government bought them a brand-new car and a house here in the U.S., that they do not have to work anymore; but in exchange for what?

"For what will it profit a man if he gains the whole world and forfeits his soul? Or what will a man give in exchange for his soul?" (Matthew 16:26)

They sell their soul to the devil, to be informants, and participate in Rwanda government espionage abroad – and in some instances, they sign up to eliminate critics by giving them poison as we will hear in the testimony of Dr Jennifer Rwamugira.

Oh poor people, they accept the cursed money, but in exchange for their soul. Recently, both Australia[4] and Canada[5] have unearthed Rwanda's alleged shadowy network of spies and their efforts to silence dissent. I am sure that in the days ahead, the U.S. and more countries will expose and destroy these terrorist groups in our midst.

Rwanda Seeking to Silence and Harm Critics Abroad

As a preacher and a human rights activist, I heard the cry of the voiceless, and my contribution has been to speak up and to be their voice. I began to bring forth basic teachings, such as "Thou Shalt Not Kill" via our TV Ministry. I also get to be invited to testify and participate in many human rights and religious freedom summits by our U.S. State Department and other organizations. This did not please the regime of Kigali. They do not want anyone who knows them to speak up. They do not want anyone to expose what is going on. They do not want any intelligent people who criticize the government.

The "Thou Shalt Not Kill"[6] series, preached in Kinyarwanda, went viral on the internet and social media. Kigali heard about it and, after numerous meetings, they decided to come close to me, to shut me down. In 2019, they created a Rwanda Diaspora in Denver. They have sought to silence me, and to threaten me, even though I bring a good message of democracy, love, unity, and the importance of respecting human rights.

In August 2018, I received a call from an unknown person. He was trying to convince me that we are both native from Rushashi, the area where my family had a farm. He went on and on, trying to convince me. I excused myself because I was in a meeting. I asked him to call the next day. I made some wise plans. When he called again, however, I saw that I was dealing with very dishonest people. People who are so nice on the outside, but inside they have plans to harm you. I noticed that each time he called, he used a different number. I later learned that this is a method used by DMI so that they cannot be tracked. If they don't want to be tracked, it is obvious they are involved in espionage and some type of suspicious activities.

A few days within that time frame, my phone company informed me that someone was trying to hack into my phone but thank God for a country like the U.S. that put safety first and protects its customers. I reported everything to local law enforcement, and they were very helpful and conducted an investigation.

Kagame Agents in my Home

In the summer of 2019, the house we live in was put on the market. It had been on the market for a while when one day, a strange new showing was requested. 24 hours are required to ready the house for a showing. The agreement was that we would leave the house for one hour during the showing.

I could have refused but for some reason, I let them in. The agent refused to give the name of who was coming which was unusual; most people give you the name when you ask. If someone seeks to enter your home and they refuse to give names, beware!

God watches over our family. God watches over our congregation, and He warned me ahead of time. He allowed this to happen so that I can write it in this book, and warn the international community. My husband happens to be a high-tech person. There is no technology out there that he does not have. He has two degrees as a network engineer, and has another one in electronics. Before we left the house, he left cameras installed in different part of the house, some hidden, some visible, with the ability to view and hear from a long distance any strange activity in our home.

I was busy with my son at the school when all of sudden my husband pulled out his app and started showing me the buyer who had requested to see the house! I could not believe with my eyes! It was a Rwandan-looking guy. Someone who is very suspicious indeed. He was physically built and one that you could tell is trained as a spy. I live in a very large home that sits on 10 acres, but a single guy coming to look at such a large estate by himself was strange in itself. I am very sure that when he arrived, he might have realized there were cameras everywhere. He avoided looking straight at the camera and walked around with his head down.

Kagame's agent in my home for an hour! No way! I quickly called the police, and by the time they got there, the man had left. Nonetheless an investigation case was opened especially that a few months before, our telephone company warned us of someone who was trying to hack into our lines.

God allowed this to happen, to remind me to never let my guard down, and to hurry up and make this matter known to all. Currently, the police patrol my home and the place where I conduct church services and business. We are not ignorant of how these evil people work, so we reported them. Some people are not able to work very well because of these death squads operating abroad, following people everywhere. I am calling forth the USA to deal with the Rwanda spies and terrorist within USA territory.

Doctor Jennifer Rwamugira is an Oncologists in Nursing. Now a Rwandan in exiled to South Africa. She was asked by DMI to spy on their behalf and as a Doctor, to give poison to Rwanda regime's opponents in South Africa.
lissakeza05@gmail.com

DR. JENNIFER RWAMUGIRA'S TRUE STORY

Doctor Jennifer Rwamugira is an Oncologist. She is now a Rwandan who fled Kagame's bloody regime and exiled to South Africa. She was approached by DMI to spy on their behalf and, as a Doctor, to give poison to the Rwanda regime's opponents in South Africa. Here is her story.

On November 3rd, 2011, I was offered a job as director of the oncology department in Rwanda Military Hospital, after completion of a master's degree from the Republic of South Africa.

On December 17th, 2011, I was given a full-time bursary to pursue a PhD in Oncology Nursing from the University of the Witwatersrand, Johannesburg, South Africa. When my employer heard about it, he was very excited. The next day he presented admission to the Ministry of Defense, after which he told me that due to the shortage of oncologists within the country, Rwanda Military Hospital, as well as the Ministry of Defense, are requesting me to do the research in Rwanda instead. Therefore, they would like to ask the university for me to attend as a part-time student. The Rwandan government would be fully responsible to pay for all the requirements, including tuition.

While checking at Kigali airport, leaving to go to South Africa for registration, I received a call from Dan Munyuza

[Everyone knows Dan Munyuza. His name is greatly feared. He is a Brigadier General who oversees assassination operations within the regime. Poisons used by the regime to kill are named after him such as Utuzi Munyuza 1, 2, etc., meaning the water they give to people, and they die within 8 hours.]

Munyuza sent someone to give me an envelope which he asked that I should submit to Dudie Rutembesa, who works at the Rwandan embassy in South Africa. I agreed and innocently found Dudie at the Johannesburg airport and gave him the envelope. Little did I know that I was carrying a message to Dudie to monitor my movements in South Africa, which he did.

On February 10th, 2012, I received a call from Lt. Col. Franco, asking about my movements and the people I am socializing with. I was shocked that they had all the details.

On February 15th, 2012, I went back to Rwanda. When I reported back at work, I was called in for questioning by the director of National Intelligence in Kigali, General Karenzi Karake, usually known as KK. I Arrived at the headquarters of National Intelligence Kimuhurura – Kigali at 9:00 a.m. I was kept waiting for five to six hours with two military guys guarding me in the office – a standard technique for showing someone exactly who is in control. The general never made any appearance, but was busy communicating to his secretary. I guessed that something was not right after I heard one of those guards saying how I betrayed the country.

As I sat waiting for KK, I sent a message to my husband, who also worked for intelligence. I grew so alarmed. My husband called Lt. Col. Franco Rutagengwa, one of KK's subordinates. "They're going to kill my wife," he said, begging for help. I was moved to Rutagengwa's office, and the questioning began. "Look here, Dr. Rwamugira..." What Rwandan intelligence (KK) wanted, the Lt. Colonel explained, was for me to help in compiling a dossier on the RNC, a Rwanda Opposition Party abroad. Franco said, "Tell us what you know about that RNC organization. Tell us what they are planning." When I pretended not to have heard of it, he slapped me and I fell down. "Cooperate with us or it'll be the worse for you," he explained.

Do as Requested by Kagame, If Not Your Family Will Perish

Lt. Col. Franco asked me about some prominent members in RNC. I responded that I don't have any clue about it. Franco's bodyguards tortured me with electrical shocks as well as hitting my head against the wall. The interrogation took place three times a week for three months. They wanted me to say that the RNC was planning to bring down the Rwanda government, setting off bombs. I told Lt. colonel Franco that I don't know anything at all, and Franco threatened me in front of my husband and Dr.

Charles Murego. "You think that you are being clever, but I want you to know that anything could happen to you!"

One day when I arrived at work, I found two RPF soldiers sitting at my computer, searching through my files. My supervisor at Wits University sent me an invitation to defend doctorate thesis in South Africa, I felt revived. Franco knew about the invitation before I did. He came to my home the night before I left. He was there till 2:00 am, trying to tell me what to do. He said they would help accommodate me in South Africa, to get close to General Kayumba, the leader of RNC and former head of intelligence in Rwanda, Colonel Patrick Karegeya. Both Kayumba and Karegeya were now both dissidents in South Africa. Rwanda wanted me to update them on their plans.

"Dr. Rwamugira, remember the whole government trusts and loves you, therefore, do as requested by His Excellence President Paul Kagame," said Franco. He gave me a scenario, how General Kayumba's father was tortured in custody and how the government took his land due to the wrongdoing of his son Kayumba. He reminded me how Colonel Karegeya's cousin was killed because of what Patrick is doing outside the country. Franco advised me to do all that is possible to fulfill the promises; otherwise, if I don't do as requested by the President of Rwanda, my family will perish. I Promised Lt. Col. Franco that I will do my best to fill full the mission as requested.

Work for Us as a Rwanda Spy

When I asked how I was supposed to communicate with him, Franco ordered a phone from Rwanda's MTN and put $150 in credit on the handset. Whenever I socialized with the RNC leadership, I should buzz him – not call – then he would be the one to call me and talk to me in my room.

Upon my arrival in South Africa, I threw away the phone instead. I informed my brother-in-law by the name of Kennedy what had happened, and I told my boss at the Rwandan Military Hospital that I would not be returning back to Rwanda. From then on, Franco would not communicate with me directly, instead, he started sending messages via my husband.

Lt. Col. Franco contacted my brother-in-law, Joseph Bagira, to persuade me to work as a Rwandan spy based in South Africa. I told them that it violated my professional code of conduct, which I am committed to. I care for the sick, to try to save lives, and not kill. Franco was reassuring, "Don't worry, you can do this, Dr. Rwamugira."

Regime Asking a Doctor to Poison People

Franco revealed the plan devised for me. It was the same scenario which had already been suggested to a fellow exile by Dan Munyuza. They said they could give me a poison to give to the opposition (RNC members). They told me, "There is nothing to fear. This poison can't be diagnosed if one gets sick. You can put it in their drink, for example, when they go to the bathroom." Franco was not too specific, as to the actual target. He said that if I could poison the entire inner circle – Kennedy, Frank, Col. Karegeya, and General Kayumba – it would be great, but the most important were General Kayumba and Col. Patrick Karegeya.

KK told my husband (William Rusakara) to cooperate with them otherwise, I will face the consequences. KK and Franco delegated one of the directors in the National Security Services (NSS), Francis Kagame, to communicate with me on their behalf. They would always do things like this, like criminals avoiding to leave behind a trace. Francis communicated via my husband's phone.

Francis sent me $500 in cash to be spent on phone credit and four new SIM Cards. He advised to alternate these in my handset on a weekly basis, in order to escape detection. After hearing all their plans, I let them know that I was unwilling to comply. They then moved on and devised an evil plan to kidnap my children, who at the time were in Uganda, but God helped us, they failed. I knew about their plans before they reached my children, and on September 26, 2012, a Good Samaritan brought my kids to South Africa.

Going After Dr. Rwamugira Extended Family Members

In August 2015, my husband, William Rusakara, was kidnapped by DMI. For more than four years, no one knew where he was held, and the family thought he had been killed. In September 2018, however, DMI agents brought Rusakara in a wheelchair, he wouldn't walk or stand. He had developed an incurable medical condition – heart disease. All his medical conditions where a result of being locked in a small confined area without being given time to exercise or stretch the body.

On the November 4th, 2018, DMI came to his mother's house, where he was staying, and took this medically frail person.

On Christmas Eve, 2019, my brother, Eddie Bagamba, was assassinated at front his gate at exactly 23:11, while coming home from an evening at Christmas prayer. The Rwandan special forces operatives, presidential guards, and selected intelligence operatives used a silencer gun and they shot him in the chest, thighs, and both legs. His head was shattered. They took the eyes out and esophagus. They tightened both arms at his back and he was thrown in the trench next to his home. The Rwandan government laid false allegations that Bagamba was assassinated due to being suspected as a Ugandan, but in truth they killed him because he is a Christian; a young man who would not compromise and take on their evil missions. He was also killed because he is related to me.

In addition, my father is being interrogated for no reason at all. His land has been confiscated. My family members are called different names, such as traitors and enemy of the county, to the extent that no one is even allowed to marry my siblings.

Appeal by Dr. Rwamugira

This is the real Rwanda. What I have shared here is what is going on in the real Rwanda. I am appealing to the United Nations. I am appealing to the American government, and to the international community:

- To demand the Rwandan government, especially President Paul Kagame, cooperate with authorities of various countries where Rwandan nationals were murdered so that justice can be done. I am appealing to you, to press Kagame to release our people in prison and to show where our family members, such my husband, are.

- To allow open political space within the country and to sit down and have dialogue with his opponents, as well as release all the political prisoners in Rwanda.

- To impose economic, political, and diplomatic sanctions to the Kigali regime until it agrees to comply with the above requirements. Remember, the budget of the Government of Rwanda is funded by taxpayers of your countries. It is through these taxes that our families, our Rwandan compatriots' brothers and sisters, are martyred. Acting on this financial incentive, you have the power to put an end to our suffering.

- To ask the United Nations Security Council to put in place an international criminal court on the DRC, to bring to justice the alleged perpetrators of war crimes, crimes against humanity, and crimes of genocide denounced in the U.N. Mapping Report on the DRC. Indeed, according to the report, the attacks during the war, from 1996-1998, and from 1998-2001, made a very large number of victims, probably by tens of thousands of members of the Hutu ethnic group, all nationalities taken together. In most of the reported cases, it is not of people killed unintentionally during fighting, but of people targeted mainly by the forces of the AFDL/APR/ FAB, executed and often stabbed. Among the victims, there was a majority of children, women, the elderly and the sick who posed no risk for the attacking forces[3]. However, until now, no national or international justice has been set up in this respect to hear those cases. This situation of impunity is certainly and directly linked to the serious violations of human rights persisting in the African Great Lakes sub-region.

INSIDE RWANDA KICUKIRO POLICE STATION

A Rwandan recounts his incarceration. His name is withheld on request for his protection.

For a month I was held at Kicukiro Police station in a tiny cell that is built in a way that you can hear all that's happening outside, but no one can hear you. There are about seven of those rooms at Kicukiro Police station, some of them holding as many as four people per room, even though one person can barely fit.

The conditions in these cells are inhumane and torturous. When one is held in there, he/she is handcuffed 24/7 arms and legs. When you go to the toilet you pass at the windows of the general population, but all other prisoners are made to lay face down so that no one can see you. On each window stands a policeman who is also not allowed to look at you. His job is to make sure no other detainee sees you. There's a unit of three people who are the only ones that are allowed to come in contact with you. They are not uniformed like other officers, and are very rude towards other officers. These are officers from the police's counterintelligence unit.

Their job is to beat you, take you for interrogations, and any other kind of torture. These are the officers who instructs you, takes you to the toilet, or to bring you food. They have no idea why you are being detained, despite torturing you. They won't ask your name or anything. They just do as they are told from above. I also believe they are the ones who do the killings when time comes.

For one month that I was there, five people were killed. All of them young boys whose crimes are common theft. There's a way we would talk under the steel doors so all of them had been there for 3 to 4 months and they knew what was coming to them, so they had made peace. They were encouraging me to be strong and just wait for my time to die. Their only prayers were that they get killed without pain.

Obviously, they had been there for long enough to know what happens there. I will never forget Muganda Bahati. They killed him a day after his birthday, on May 2, 2019. He told me he had turned 21. He told me he grew up as a street kid, and he'd been arrested many times.

If DMI or counterintelligence police get tired of arresting an individual, they kidnap him and hold him in secret. If no one asks about him, they kill him. The other five guys didn't say much. I suspect they were there for political reasons. If one can enter in one of those rooms. you will be terrified merely by the writings on the walls of these execution waiting cells. Every prisoner leaves a footprint in there. Its horrifying.

My ordeal is long and obviously not as bad as other fellow Rwandans are suffering but I decided I will be doing all I can to let people know what's going on in that country. Innocent people are being killed simply for nothing, totally for nothing. For example, I was never in politics or ever criticized the government, but someone reported me to the authority on things that I didn't do or say. But at Kicukiro police station, I was able to see and hear stories which are still haunting me.

12

RWANDA HOPE

The book of Apocalypse is the final book of the Bible. It is a book full of mysteries, prediction and revelation of future events that lead into the second coming of Jesus Christ. It was written in a time of crisis, in the face of ruthless persecution by fierce dictators and adversaries of Christians. Among them Emperor Nero who, in 64 A.D., arrested and tortured Christians to death. Those who proclaimed the truth faced the fury of satan's most vicious attacks, suffering, intense testing and even death by martyrdom. Those who killed had nothing to fear from the law, in fact it was as though they were carrying out the law.

The book of Apocalypse is an intense book that reveals seven years of tribulation and the final showdown between good and evil. Believers are to take courage and persevere. The end has no "Dead End" for those who choose life over death.

Christ has triumphed over satan, and ultimately, He will return to vindicate the chosen, forever destroying wickedness, leading truth and justice to victory.

In conclusion, good triumphs over evil. He who laughs last laughs best.

The Good News for Rwandans

The good news is that evil will never win. He who chooses lies over the truth chooses to build his house on the sand. When the time comes for the storm to roll in, when the waves come up, that house will collapse. So, in the end, with the test of time, what's built by means of evil will fall.

Dear oppressed Rwandans, though your voice was stolen and though you might not have powerful lobbyists to lobby for you, and though you might not know how to rally powerful men behind you, remember that you have God behind you. If you have the truth as your belt, God stands strong by your side. God told me to tell you, "You are blessed because when you stand on the truth, the ground all around you will shake. Everything will fall all around you and the mountains will crumble, but you will stand strong, because you stand with Me."

So, the good news is that evil does not have the last say. God has the last say! In the end, good will win over evil. Evil might win some battles, but only good wins the war.

Learning from History

- The book of the Maccabees tells us a story of a man named Jason, a corrupted priest who sold his soul to kill his own people "For his part, Jason continued the merciless slaughter of his fellow citizens, not realizing that triumph over one's own kindred is the greatest calamity. He thought he was winning a victory over his enemies, not over his own people." What was Jason's end? "And he who had cast out so many to lie unburied went unmourned and without a funeral of any kind, nor any place in the tomb of his ancestors." 2 Maccabees 5:6, 10

- During the time of the Pharaohs in Egypt, the Bible tells us of a king who rose to oppress the children of Israel. He afflicted them with hard labor. "But the more they afflicted them, the more they multiplied and the more they spread out, so that they were in dread of the sons of Israel." (Exodus 1:12). It is unfortunate that a ruler can choose to lord it over His people with an iron fist, but even if this happens, it is to not lose heart. Even in time of such distress, God caused His people to multiply. Out of evil, God birthed something wonderful. This evil did not work for Pharaoh, so he came with other evil plans, "and he said, 'When you are helping the Hebrew women to give birth and see *them* upon the birthstool, if it is a son, then you shall put him to death; but if it is a daughter, then she shall live.' " (Exodus 1:16) "Every son who is born you are to cast into the Nile, and every daughter you are to keep alive." Exodus 1:22 But still evil did not win. Moses survived and in due time, God delivered His people from the hand of the oppressor. And he who cast many children into the Nile ended up being cast into the red sea with his entire army, the evil one to be found no more. Evil did not win back then, and evil will not win today.

- During the times of the Maccabees, there came a certain Antiochus Epiphanes, an evil king who shed much blood of the Jewish people. He abolished the Jewish religion and desecrated the temple of God. He built pagan altars, sacrificed swine and unclean animals in the holy place where he erected the abomination of desolation upon the altar. Epiphanes burned the holy scriptures and put to death anyone who refused to bend to his laws. Did he win? History tells us that he met a miserable end. He who had cast out so many to lie unburied was struck with sickness of extreme sufferings and died in a foreign land. (2 Mac 9:28-29)

- Time and time again, history has taught us that light wins over darkness. Look at Hitler – Under his leadership and racially motivated ideology, six million Jews were destroyed. His Nazi ideology won momentarily, but in the end, God caused good to triumph over evil. Hitler ended in ruin, for he who destroys his people only destroys himself. Today, Hitler is not celebrated, nor is he mourned.

Yes, from 1990, Rwanda plunged into a 30-year apocalypse, which received no significant coverage in the media. At times when there was coverage, the story was told by the oppressors. Instead of telling the truth, they lied and blinded people with Kigali, the cleanest city in Africa and according to Rwanda, the cleanest in the whole world! The great city, there is none like it! Many gave praises and turned a blind eye on those mourning inside the city. For 30 years, in our modern history, Rwandans watched their loved ones being brutally murdered. There seemed to be no help at all to stop these atrocities. In time of adversity, when refuges were being slaughtered, though the witnesses spoke up and sent SOS messages, there was silence from international community. Rwandans were forsaken. Rwanda's voice was given no attention.

In the past, when the 1994 genocide took place, all the help to come and stop it were blocked. When the democide took place for 30 years, all help was blocked, no one believed, and no one came to the rescue of Rwandans. According to the scripture:

Justice is turned back,

And righteousness stands far away;

For truth has stumbled in the street,

And uprightness cannot enter.

Yes, truth is lacking;

And he who turns aside from evil makes himself a prey.

Now the LORD saw,

And it was displeasing in His sight that there was no justice.

And He saw that there was no man,

And was astonished that there was no one to intercede;

Then His own arm brought salvation to Him,

And His righteousness upheld Him.

(Isaiah 59:14-16)

During the atrocities of 1994, when no one came, God came for His people. When no one rescued, God came and rescued. Even now, God will rescue the enslaved and oppressed Rwandans. Even in what seems to be impossible situation, miracles still happen today. There is no cliff too high or too steep; no pit too deep, no ditch too narrow that God cannot use and make a way to rescue his people. No matter the bad situation Rwanda is in right now, no matter where Rwanda is today, whether in the deep water, in the midst of the fire, in the pit —God is mightily coming for her. Where all else fails, God prevails.

Christ in You, the Hope of Glory

"As it was in the beginning, so shall it be in the end." We are standing at the crossroad where history will repeat itself. Queen Kanjogera and King Musinga obtained power by treachery and through the shedding of much blood[1]. When the Gospel was presented to them, they rejected the Gospel, and chose evil over good. In November 1931, Musinga who had obtained the power by illegitimate means was deposed by the Belgian administration and replaced by his own son Mutara Rudahigwa[2]. In the end, Queen Kanjogera and King Musinga reaped what they had sown. Rudahigwa accepted the good news. He believed and he became the first Rwandan king to be baptized. On Sunday, October 27, 1946, in Nyanza, King Rudahigwa, kneeling at the foot of the altar dedicated Rwanda to Christ the King with a powerful prayer.[3] [4] Christ in you, the hope of glory (Colossians 1:27).

The story of Rwanda monarchy did not end with Rwanda without Christ. Rwanda has Christ in her heart. Rwanda will be free from dictatorship. Rwanda, the heart of Africa, will have a great revival. Killings, abductions, tortures, incarceration, and all abomination will forever be abolished in Rwanda. That time has come. That time is now.

FINAL PLEA - SOS

Save Our Soul! Rwandans have been sold to dictatorship.
Save Our Soul! Rwandans have been sold to be destroyed.
Save Our Soul! Rwandans have been sold to be massacred and eliminated.

Rwandans are not asking for a land. Rwandans are not

asking for aid. Rwandans are not asking for even a single dollar. Rwandans are not asking for material things. What Rwandans are asking right now, above all things else, beyond the aid, beyond the dollar, Rwandans are asking for their own lives. Give Rwandans their lives.

Rwandans are hostages in their own country. Open the borders. If people cannot have a life in their country, help them flee. Set them free from Kagame's hostage. Rwandans inside the enclave cry in unison: SOS

Save Our Soul!

May their prayer be answered.

FOOTNOTES

———

SOS

1. https://www.un.org/en/preventgenocide/rwanda/historical-background.shtml

Chapter 1

1. Alison Des Forges, "Defeat Is the Only Bad News: Rwanda under Musinga, 1896–1931"
2. Judi Rever, "In Praise of Blood: The Crimes of the Rwandan Patriotic Front"
3. https://www.penguinrandomhouse.com/books/546081/in-praise-of-blood-by-judi-rever/

Chapter 2

1. Um'Khonde Habamenshi. www.umkhonde.org
2. https://youtu.be/5zLP9HcVBEs
3. https://medium.com/@david.himbara_27884
4. https://www.bbc.com/news/world-africa-25713774
5. Voice recording by Kizito Mihigo's friend who lives in France and chose to remain anonymous

Chapter 3

1. Barafinda YouTube Channel: https://youtu.be/LrsjsSXZBEI
   Barafinda Facebook: https://www.facebook.com/imbwa.icumi

2. https://medium.com/@david.himbara_27884/kagame-spreading-propaganda-via-advertorials-in-us-media-3938c97a8cfb

Chapter 4

1. J. J. Carney (2011). From Democratization to Ethnic Revolution: Catholic Politics in Rwanda, 1950-1962 (Ph.D). Catholic University of America. pp. 62–63.
2. https://religionnews.com/2018/03/07/rwanda-closes-hundreds-of-churches-and-arrests-pastors/

Chapter 5

1. https://www.un.org/en/preventgenocide/rwanda/historical-background.shtml
2. https://en.wikipedia.org/wiki/Rwandan_Revolution
3. https://en.wikipedia.org/wiki/Fred_Rwigyema
4. https://www.un.org/en/preventgenocide/rwanda/historical-background.shtml
5. https://en.wikipedia.org/wiki/Rwandan_Revolution
6. https://en.wikipedia.org/wiki/Rosalie_Gicanda
7. https://www.orwelltoday.com/readerrwandaqueen.shtml
8. Friend of Reason: https://www.facebook.com/groups/171709199555433/permalink/751105511615796/
9. https://www.jambonews.net/en/actualites/20180402-honouring-all-assassinated-political-figures-a-step-towards-achieving-a-solid-reconciliation-in-rwanda/

10. https://www.jambonews.net/en/actualites/20180402-honouring-all-assassinated-political-figures-a-step-towards-achieving-a-solid-reconciliation-in-rwanda/

Chapter 6

1. https://www.jambonews.net/en/actualites/20180402-honouring-all-assassinated-political-figures-a-step-towards-achieving-a-solid-reconciliation-in-rwanda/
2. https://www.jambonews.net/en/actualites/20180402-honouring-all-assassinated-political-figures-a-step-towards-achieving-a-solid-reconciliation-in-rwanda/
3. https://medium.com/search?q=Kagame%20Said%20It%20Was%20Too%20Late%20Toto%20Stop%20Genocide
4. https://www.jambonews.net/en/actualites/20190416-rwanda-i-would-like-my-pain-to-be-recognized/
5. https://www.jta.org/2018/01/29/israel/israel-backs-un-resolution-on-name-change-for-rwanda-genocide-opposed-by-us
6. www.christinecoleman.org
7. https://medium.com/@david.himbara_27884
8. https://www.hrw.org/reports/1999/rwanda/Geno15-8-03.htm

Chapter 7

1. Espérance Mukashema (2016). "They Killed an Angel, My Last Born Son Richard Sheja." Editions la Pagaie.

Chapter 9

1. https://www.ohchr.org/EN/Countries/AfricaRegion/Pages/DRCUNMappingReport.aspx
2. www.theblazingholyfire.com
3. http://perewenceslas.centerblog.net/rub-L-EGLISE-DU-RWANDA-VICTIME.html
4. https://en.wikipedia.org/wiki/Christophe_Munzihirwa_Mwene_Ngabo

Chapter 10

1. https://en.wikipedia.org/wiki/Kibeho_massacre
2. Ann Garrison. https://www.youtube.com/watch?v=elACfHBVvXA
3. https://www.ntnews.com.au/news/northern-territory/australian-troops-remember-kibeho-massacre-in-rwanda/news-story/1c6be840029a30cb1be26b0f3b96242c
4. http://www.mdrwi.org/rapports%20et%20doc/utuntu%20utuntu/indahiroyarpf.htm

Chapter 11

1. https://en.wikipedia.org/wiki/Paul_Rusesabagina
2. Rusesabagina, Paul (2006). An Ordinary Man. The Penguin Group
3. https://www.youtube.com/channel/UCaEcrM1rQQToNT3EqIEVnfw

4. https://www.abc.net.au/news/2019-08-25/spies-in-our-suburbs-alleged-spy-web-silencing-rwandan-refugees/11317704

5. https://ici.radio-canada.ca/info/2019/10/espionnage-rwanda-gouvernement-canada-paul-kagame/ https://youtu.be/RPm3WAEEG3o

6. youtube.com/c/GDVKLRwanda

Chapter 12

1. Alison Des Forges, "Defeat Is the Only Bad News: Rwanda under Musinga, 1896–1931"

2. https://en.wikipedia.org/wiki/Mutara_III_Rudahigwa

3. Aimable Twagilimana , "Historical Dictionary of Rwanda"

4. http://historyofafricaotherwise.blogspot.com/2011/10/lithuania-rwanda-jesus-christ-inducted.html

ABOUT THE AUTHOR

Reverend Christine Coleman is a writer, motivational speaker, televangelist, and the founding pastor of Blazing Holy Fire Church. A native of Rwanda, Christine migrated to the United States in 1997, following the genocide and wars that ravaged the Great Lakes Region. She is an activist and has been anointed by the Lord to pray and minister to heads of state and world influencers. In May 2017, she was one of the nation's faith leaders who joined President Trump at the White House as he signed an executive order to protect religious liberty. Christine is married to Michael Coleman. They have one son, Christian, and make their home in the Rocky Mountains.

ChristineColeman.org

Printed in Great Britain
by Amazon